Weekly Devotionals from the

E-Mail Series

Thirsty Thursdays™

"...Do not get drunk on wine, which leads to debauchery. Instead, be filled with the Spirit."

Ephesians 5:17-20

Rev. Marcus D. King

RMC INTERNATIONAL
Arlington, Texas

Weekly Devotionals from the Thirsty Thursday E-Mail Series™

ISBN 0-9728437-0-1

Cover Design By Jack Akana Jr.

Edited By Tandra Johnson

Published By
RMC International
P.O. Box 183871
Arlington, TX 76096

Acknowledgements

To God the Father, Son, and Holy Spirit for the gift of grace that enabled me to write these devotionals.

†††

To my father and mother for being models of Jesus by their lifestyle. And to Renae McMillan who was the only one patient enough to push me to finish this work. Thanks Renae for your inspiration. May all who drink from the Word of Life be filled and never thirst again.

†††

There are many people who have invested in me and encouraged me. I want to thank you all for there are too many of you to name! To name a few my pastor Frederick D. Haynes, III, Dr. E.K. Bailey, my brother and sister Rev. Eric and Regina King, and the entire Friendship West Baptist Church family. I love you all!

Table of Contents

Table of Contents

Table of Contents

Table of Contents

WEEK ONE

Who Has The Best Plan?

Scripture

Jeremiah 29:11 "For I know the plans I have for you," says the Lord.

◆◆◆◆◆◆◆◆◆◆◆◆◆◆◆◆◆◆◆

Where do you see yourself in five years? 10 years? How many children do you want? When are you going to buy that house? Get into a relationship? Get married? These questions, among others, are asked to us more often than we would like. Sometimes, it seems to make you rush into certain areas just to shut people up! May I ask you a question? Thanks for your permission. Are there some things that you planned in your life that didn't go as planned? If so, welcome to orientation. Orientation? Yes! This is the introduction to God's Plan Is Better Than Your Plan University (GPIBTYPU). The first semester, you will take such courses as "Better Choices, Recovering From Poor Planning," and our most intriguing course "Waiting on An Answer From God Before You Take Matters Into Your Own Hands." You need these classes, because they will help you to not make the same mistakes again in the future. Each student will be issued a Bible and a helmet. The Bible is to give directions in life. The helmet is to soften the blows to the

◆◆◆◆

"The steps of a good man are ordered by the Lord."

◆◆◆◆

head when you're disobedient and go the wrong way. Follow the Map! There is more than one way to get to Africa from the U.S., but why swim when there are boats and airplanes available? God knows where you're going even if you don't. He knows how to get you there. Why take risks in drowning with your plan when He can take you another way? Maybe what you've been planning has nothing to do with Him. If so, ask Him today what His plans are for you. If you refuse to do so, you really do need that helmet, because you're going to have a lot of headaches from running into walls. "The steps of a good man are ordered by the Lord." Be careful where you put your feet. Make sure they are pointed in the right direction before you start walking.

◆◆◆◆◆◆◆◆◆◆◆◆◆◆◆◆◆◆◆◆

Prayer

Dear Lord, what is your plan for my life? I have plans and goals, but show me what your plans and goals are. I just want your will. You know what's best for me. Help me heal from past choices, and help me create some better ones for my future. I want your plan. Please close the doors that I don't need to walk through, and open the doors I need to walk into. Then, give me the strength to go in. In Jesus name I pray, Amen.

WEEK TWO

Love Her Right!

Scripture

Ephesians 5:25 "And you husbands must love your wives with the same love Christ showed the church."

◆ ◆ ◆ ◆ ◆ ◆ ◆ ◆ ◆ ◆ ◆ ◆ ◆ ◆ ◆ ◆ ◆ ◆ ◆ ◆

Are you a husband or a husband in training? Then there are some things God says to us as men on how to treat the women we are in relationships with. Are you ready for them? I Corinthians 13:4-8 helps us out too. Love her like Jesus loves the church! Okay, let me give you an example. Love is not irritable. When she wants to talk, do you listen? Do you listen without trying to fix her situation? Your listening ear can be her solution, because she just wants her man to let her talk out her feelings. Do you take the time to tell her she's beautiful without having a hidden agenda? Love is kind. Do you let things from the past go? Love keeps no record of when it has been wronged. Do you walk out of the room instead of working through your problem when she has an issue with something, or do you give her the respect you want when you have an issue? Do you say it's your way or the highway or make decisions and tell her about them later when they involve the both of you? Love does not demand its own way (verbal or non-verbal), Do you complain when she is slow in getting to places without trying to help her get there on time? Do you verbally abuse her and make her feel inadequate? Have you given up on her in some areas even though you're still in a rela-

◆ ◆ ◆ ◆

"Love keeps no record of when it has been wronged."

◆ ◆ ◆ ◆

tionship with her? Love: never gives up, never loses faith, is always hopeful, and endures through every circumstance. Do you talk to her like she's one of your boys, or are you gentle with your speech and choose your words carefully, because you know she's not a roughneck, she's a rose? Death and Life are in the power of the tongue! " Don't crush her. Build her up. She's more than her looks, job, perfume, legs, thighs, breasts, lips, hips. She's a queen. If you don't know how to treat a queen, then maybe you don't need to try to live in the palace! Are you loving your woman like Jesus does the church? Sacrifice, forgive, be patient; even when you may be right or she may be getting on your nerves with her mood swings. Spend time with her when she needs you. If you don't love her right, God has someone who will. Don't wait until things fall apart before you recognize who you have. Be a man and do like Jesus. We were wrong, but he came to us to make it right, because he loved us more than His pride. Are you loving her right brother? If you don't, some other man will.

◆◆◆◆◆◆◆◆◆◆◆◆◆◆◆◆◆◆◆

Prayer

Dear Jesus, it's hard trying to love like you. I ask that every man take the challenge seriously that you have given us. You have given us the privilege to share with beautiful, sensitive, strong women. Help us be what they need whether we are married or one day hope to be. Thank you for showing us your love. Now teach us how to give it. Amen.

WEEK THREE

Soup or Steak!

Scripture

Proverbs 15:17 "A bowl of soup with someone you love is better than steak with someone you hate."

May I ask you a question? Thanks for your permission. What is your measure of a good relationship? I mean relationships with parents, friends, etc. I think many times we focus on what we don't have and miss the important things in life. You may not make a million dollars (steak), but you have a job that God has blessed you with that takes care of your needs (soup). You may not have the house like your friends (steak), but you have a nice place to lay your head when others are on the street (soup). Your man or your woman may not make the money you always dreamed they would (steak), but you have fun together; they are faithful, and you like spending time with them (soup). What is considered steak (a real meal), and what is considered soup (cheaper, not as fancy) in your life? May I give you some help? Do you ask for steak or soup when you have a cold? Is it steak or soup that you purchase when you are low on your money? Soup is with you when the times are hard. Soup is with you regardless of your financial income. Soup nurses you back to health when you're sick. All I'm trying to say is.... what we think is important really isn't that important. Find someone who loves you for you. Find someone who loves

"Soup nurses you back to health when you're sick."

you for who you are. Find someone who wants what's best for you. They may make soup money, but they have the work habits and giving heart of a steak. They may be tough and have your back like a steak. Ask God to remind you and show you the people who you consider soup friends. These are people you can depend on. Then ask Him to show you the things in your life that you consider soup (less valuable) that many others wish they had but don't. You need someone to eat soup with in your life. Why? When you get old that's all you'll be able to eat anyway. Get some practice now! Listen to this, "If you're faithful over a few things (soup), I'll make you ruler over many (steak)." Matthew 25:21 Eat your soup and be thankful, and God will upgrade you to a steak "Be Thankful," Chapter 1 verse 1 from the Marcus King James Version of the Bible. He may even change your soup into a steak. Be careful who and what you pass up because it doesn't look like much right now! Tell your soupy friends and relatives who have been tough and strong for you like a steak "THANK YOU" today.

◆◆◆◆◆◆◆◆◆◆◆◆◆◆◆◆◆◆◆◆

Prayer

Dear Lord, Thank you for showing me that real value is in commitment, love, and sacrifice. Thank you for having people in my life that have shown commitment to me, loved me, and have sacrificed for me. Bless all of them who I may even have forgotten about. Bless those I don't even know about. Thank you for what I do have. Even these things I don't deserve! In Jesus' name I pray, amen.

WEEK FOUR

Be Alert!

Scripture

I Peter 5:8-9 "Be careful! Watch out for attacks from the devil, your great enemy. He prowls around like a roaring lion, looking for some victim to devour."

◆◆◆◆◆◆◆◆◆◆◆◆◆◆◆◆◆◆◆◆

When you do good and try to live right, expect conflict! When you pray, expect an answer, but also expect a decoy before the real thing comes along. Why? The devil hears your prayers too. He can't stop you from getting them answered, but he can distract you for a while and have you chasing, or holding on to the wrong thing. Expect people to trip when you're feeling good. This is not preparation for negative results in your life. Not at all. This is being realistic about the opposition that faces you. Satan! He hates the fact that you are making changes, praying for changes, and praying for changes for the better for those around you. You can't change with-

◆◆◆◆◆◆

"...So look for that joker to show up in your job, family, finances, relationships."

◆◆◆◆◆◆

out changing the devil's place in your life. He does have a place in your life. That place is to help fulfill God's plan for your life. Huh? Yeah, God uses him to frustrate you; then you turn to God, and God takes you to another level. Remember, the devil is God's devil. He can't do a thing without God allowing him to. So look for that joker to show up in your job, family, finances, relationships. When he shows up, turn to God, then God will help you place him under your feet. You will walk on what used to make you frustrated. Keep your eyes open for blessings and challenges. The two mixed together make a good Christian.

◆◆◆◆◆◆◆◆◆◆◆◆◆◆◆◆◆◆◆◆

Prayer

Dear Lord, thanks for having my back on the things I can't see, as well as those things I can. Help me not to get depressed, become fearful, or let others control me. Protect me from evil. Help me see attacks before they come so that I can make adjustments. Thanks Jesus.

WEEK FIVE

The Little Things

Scripture

Luke 16:10 "Unless you are faithful in small matters, you won't be faithful in large ones. If you cheat even a little, you won't be honest with greater responsibilities."

◆◆◆◆◆◆◆◆◆◆◆◆◆◆◆◆◆◆◆◆

When you pray, I mean really pray, God will begin to show you who you really are. People make me laugh when they say they are close to God, but yet they have this holier than thou attitude. If you are close to God, you know that there are areas where you struggle, and other Christians struggle as well. For instance, are you a better, stronger Christian because you don't drink, struggle with sex, or struggle with jealousy? I don't think so! Those who frown on others' struggles need to take heed, lest that very struggle become theirs. A real saint of God knows that the little things make the difference to God. Your title of Elder, Bishop, Apostle, Pastor, choir leader, or custodian does not put you above struggle. Those who think so are either not being real with themselves, or they are not reading their Bibles correctly. David struggled,

◆◆◆◆◆◆

"A real saint of God knows that the little things make the difference to God."

◆◆◆◆◆◆

Paul struggled, even Jesus struggled in the garden with his fleshly desires. Who are we then? Are we more anointed, better, more important? What small things are tripping you up from going to the next level? Are you being honest in all that you say and do? Are you witnessing to every person God tells you to? Are you spending the time with God that He asks you to? Are you being obedient to EVERY THING God is saying do? What is your attitude like today? Are you judging and gossiping about your brother or sister instead of praying for them and helping them? If not, that means there's room for improvement! Thank God for His grace to help us. It's not there to take advantage of, but it sure has blessed me to get where I am today. It's the little things friend, the little things. One thing done right at a time adds up to and pays for the big thing that you want. It's time to get to work on that thing the Spirit has pointed out today! Your destiny awaits you.

◆ ◆ ◆ ◆ ◆ ◆ ◆ ◆ ◆ ◆ ◆ ◆ ◆ ◆ ◆ ◆ ◆ ◆ ◆

Prayer

Dear Jesus, forgive me of my sins. Show me my faults. Give me strength to obey in the little things. Thanks for your help Jesus. You know I need it. In Jesus name I pray, Amen.

WEEK SIX

If They Only Knew!

Scripture

John 7:41 Others said, "He is the Messiah." Still others said, "But He can't be! Will the Messiah come from Galilee?"

◆◆◆◆◆◆◆◆◆◆◆◆◆◆◆◆◆◆◆◆

Are you trying to prove yourself to someone? Do people know who you really are? Listen friend, some people counted Jesus out. They said He couldn't be great because of where He came from, where He lived. A lot of times God uses people who have started with nothing, were thought of as nothing, looked like nothing, talked like nothing, and made them SOMETHING! God Majors in the Minors. Don't waste another day spending your energy on people who don't know who you are. If they don't believe you because you say it, then it just may be too late for them when they see it. Their loss! If they only knew how caring you were. If they only knew the vision God has given you for your life. If they only knew that you had been practicing while everyone else was playing. If they only knew that your showing up and being faithful is being neglected by your boss but is being monitored by God. If they only knew that the blessing they feel

◆◆◆◆◆

"It takes a special person to be second in command when you know you are first in anointing."

◆◆◆◆◆

you aren't ready for, you've already been destined to have. If they only knew that you were the head and not the tail. It takes a special person to be second in command when you know you are first in anointing. That's where God is building your character. Learn where you are. God will soon raise you up. If they only knew that you make more money than they thought! If they only knew that God has plans, BIG Plans for you. Ya'll talked about it, and He didn't forget it. Walk around today knowing who you are; knowing you are royalty; knowing your income doesn't determine your outcome; knowing your past doesn't cancel your future. Be thankful for where God has blessed you to be. It could be a whole lot different. **Tell someone today, "If you only knew!"**

◆ ◆ ◆ ◆ ◆ ◆ ◆ ◆ ◆ ◆ ◆ ◆ ◆ ◆ ◆ ◆ ◆ ◆ ◆

Prayer

Dear Jesus, thank you for having a future for me. I thank you for my present, because you are building me to handle my future. Help me love who you made me to be, even if others can't see what I'm worth. You have made me a little lower than the angels. That means you took time when you made me. I'm a work of Art. As long as I know you are the artist, you can paint anything into my life when you get ready. Paint a blessing or two. I don't mind. I love you Jesus. Amen.

WEEK SEVEN

How Much Love Do You Have?

Scripture

John 15:12-13 "I command you to love each other in the same way that I love you. And here is how to measure it-the greatest love is shown when people lay down their lives for their friends"

◆◆◆◆◆◆◆◆◆◆◆◆◆◆◆◆◆◆◆◆

Everyone loves Valentine's Day. We like the hearts, gifts, flowers, and romance. But what about the LOVE? I think we as humans get special days mixed up. This is a day to show love. It should be a day of celebration for what we do all year long. How much love do you have? Real love is the love Jesus gives. It loves through good and bad. It is so strong and so abundant that it will go as far as to die for those it cares deeply about. Look around you and see who you are willing to die for. To lay down your life also means to lay down your agenda, your feelings, and what you feel and help a friend to feel loved. It shortens the list of those you truly love like Jesus doesn't it? Think of how unlovely we are at times. Think of how unlovely we were before we knew Him, yet He loved us before we even knew Him. He loved us so much that He did die for us! If that is the standard for loving, I'll be honest and say, "I have a lot of growing to do." It's hard to love those who do you wrong or who don't agree with you. It's easy to love when it's convenient. I don't think Jesus' death was convenient! He didn't ask us

◆◆◆◆◆

"..know that if you don't feel loved today, Jesus "Got Much Love For Ya!"

◆◆◆◆◆

to love like Him, He told us to (No Option if we say we are a Christian). How much love do you have for those in your life? I'm sure if you're like me, you have a lot of growing to do. Just know that if you don't feel loved today, Jesus "Got Much Love For Ya!" He always shows you. Can you read this devotional? That's Love! Can you breathe? That's Love! Love gives you things when you don't deserve them. How much love do you have this Valentine's Day? We can't base our love on how we feel. We'd be in trouble if God felt that way about us. Do you need to show love today? Do it! Somebody needs your smile, a kind word, a little note, a thank you, a hand shake, a hug, a pat on the back. Don't be so concerned about yourself today. Give love away, and it will come back to you more than you could ever imagine..."Give and it shall be given unto you, good measure, pressed down, shaken together, and running over shall men give unto to you." (Luke 6:38) You have to give in order to receive in God's love economy. Are you ready? If this day goes by and you don't smile, it could be because you didn't muster up enough strength in your face to give one.

◆ ◆ ◆ ◆ ◆ ◆ ◆ ◆ ◆ ◆ ◆ ◆ ◆ ◆ ◆ ◆ ◆ ◆ ◆

Prayer

Dear Lord, help me love when I don't feel like loving. You said do it, so help me. When I think of what you've loved me through, I can't stop loving you. Let someone see your love through me today so they can experience your love, too. It's so good that I just have to give it away. Thanks Jesus, and forgive me for not loving people as I should. In Jesus' name I pray, Amen

WEEK EIGHT

Is God Pleased?

Scripture

Genesis 4: 4-5 "The Lord accepted Abel and his offering, but He did not accept Cain and his offering. This made Cain very angry and dejected."

◆◆◆◆◆◆◆◆◆◆◆◆◆◆◆◆◆◆◆◆

Is God really pleased with what we give Him? God did not accept Cain, nor what Cain had to offer. Man, what do you think of that? Does that mean that we can say we are going to church, giving a little offering, and God is not impressed at all? You'd better believe it! Abel gave God a good offering. He gave like Cain from the produce of his work, but he gave his best. Cain just gave God whatever he picked up. My question today to you is, "Is God pleased with what you say you are giving to Him?" You go to church, but are you involved in and working in a ministry? You give in the offering, but does it reflect what you really are able to give? God rejected Cain and his offering, because Cain wasn't in the mindset when he gave to God. As a result, God rejected him and his pitiful little thing he called a "sacrifice." Do we really know what a sacrifice is? Ask Jesus. He does. It's when you give of yourself even when it is not convenient, because

◆◆◆◆◆

"We fail to sacrifice our time for others because we have forgotten who sacrificed for us."

◆◆◆◆◆

you remember that Christ died an "inconvenient death." We fail to sacrifice our time for others, because we have forgotten who sacrificed for us. You say, "I got to where I am without anyone's help!" If you really think that friend, you are foolish, blind, and have a severe case of amnesia! Oh, and God ain't pleased! How can I do something to please God? "Without **faith** it is impossible to please God." (Hebrews 11:6) Believe what God says....**every word.** Give of your time to help in your church. Give of your money in a way that reflects what God has done for you. **TITHE!** Give a tenth of your time doing something for someone else. Are you ready for an opportunity to do so?

◆ ◆ ◆ ◆ ◆ ◆ ◆ ◆ ◆ ◆ ◆ ◆ ◆ ◆ ◆ ◆ ◆ ◆ ◆

Prayer

Dear Lord, thank you for all you have done for me. Help me remember what I have and how I got to where I am. You brought me here. Because you brought me here, help me to give my time, my money, and my support. Forgive me for where I have missed it. Help me do only what you would have me to do. Give me wisdom of what I should and should not get involved in so I can be in your will. I just want to please you. In Jesus' name I pray, Amen.

WEEK NINE

From Visions to Reality

Scripture

Habakkuk 2:2-3 Then the Lord said to me," Write my answer in large, clear letters on a tablet. so that a runner can read it and tell everyone else. But these things I plan won't happen right away. Slowly, steadily, surely, the time approaches when the vision will be fulfilled."

◆◆◆◆◆◆◆◆◆◆◆◆◆◆◆◆◆◆◆◆

Are you waiting for an answer from God? If so, you should take notes on Every sermon, Every bible study, Every devotion that you participate in, because He said "write it down on a tablet." God speaks, but do we miss our answers because we take the day off, or we are unprepared to receive His answer? God will answer you! Just because He answers, doesn't mean that is the time to move on what He answered. There's a difference between "revelation" and "implementation." You see, just because God shows you what He wants you to do or have doesn't mean the timing is right for you to act on it. He may have to work some things out first so you can be ready for it, and it will be ready for you. He lets us have a "peak" at our future. If you

◆◆◆◆◆

"He may have to work some things out first so you can be ready for it and it will be ready for you... "

◆◆◆◆◆

ever see a peak, get ready for God to start moving stuff around, taking stuff away, adding things here, frustrating you there. Why? He has to work you into shape so you can handle what He showed you. That my friend will take you through a process, which will take some time. How long? I don't know. But I do know that the quicker you submit to what God wants, and the quicker you get your ideas and what you think is best for you out of the way, the quicker your Vision will become a Reality. Now Sip on that one for a while!

◆◆◆◆◆◆◆◆◆◆◆◆◆◆◆◆◆◆◆◆

Prayer

Dear Lord, I want what you want. Help me get out of the way. Help me look for an answer when I have prayed. Then, help me be patient to wait on what you have promised or shown me. Most importantly, help me not try to help you out in order to try to bring the vision you give me to pass. You don't need my help. Just show me what to do while I wait. In Jesus' name I pray, amen!

WEEK TEN

Signs that a Blessing is Near

Scripture

Luke 1:30 "Don't be afraid, Mary," the angel told her, "for God has decided to bless you!"

◆◆◆◆◆◆◆◆◆◆◆◆◆◆◆◆◆◆◆◆

When the angel Gabriel came to Mary, she became confused and disturbed, because this had never happened to her before. Then the angel told her that she would become pregnant. *Now you know that hadn't happened before.* God had chosen to bless her, but she was **confused**, **afraid**, and **disturbed!** Could it be friend that you are about to receive a blessing you never prayed for that is greater than anything you could imagine? Before her blessing came, Mary was first introduced to someone she didn't know (**An angel**), had feelings that were negative emotions (**confusion, fear, uncomfortable**), and was given assurance that her life would change because the Holy Spirit would help these things come to pass (**vs. 35).** Friend, could it be that God has decided to bless you? Trust me. What He's about to do in your life will make you forget

◆◆◆◆◆

"Winter is passing by and Spring is just around the corner. Aren't you ready to blossom?"

◆◆◆◆◆

the pain you went through. **Every season must change.** Winter is passing by and **Spring** is just around the corner. Aren't you ready to blossom? It's almost time! Jesus was her blessing. He not only blessed her, but others as well. That's the kind of blessing you are about to receive. It's bigger than you. Do you believe that? I speak that into your life this day! God's about to get you pregnant with something that will be a blessing for years to come! The only way you get pregnant is by being intimate. Make sure you are close to Him!

◆◆◆◆◆◆◆◆◆◆◆◆◆◆◆◆◆◆◆

Prayer

Dear Lord, I pray that you help everyone believe that you are changing the season of their life for the better. I pray that they recognize the angels you send their way. Help them discern between your angels and the angels of Satan. I thank you for discernment, and I thank you for a new season in their lives. I thank you for giving them a reason to enjoy their day...**hope**! In Jesus' name I pray, amen.

WEEK ELEVEN

What's In Your Garden?

Scripture

Galatians 6:7 "You will always reap what you sow."

The word **reap** means "to obtain a return or reward." This verse tells us that whatever we put out will eventually come back to us. Think about that for a second. Usually we think of this scripture in a negative sense, yet it is positive as well. Basically, whatever effort you put out when working for someone, whatever attitude you display around people, however you treat people you like and don't like, whatever you say about people, will all come back to you one day. **Now here is the key thing to remember:** *you don't know when it will come back, nor from which direction it will always come.* I like that part! That means if I have been making peace come in others lives; if I have been giving to God in my time of plenty and in times when finances are not so plentiful; if I have been consistent in doing a task even when I didn't feel like it, but did it because I knew I was serving God; if I show love even when I don't feel like I am being loved properly, ALL OF THAT WILL ONE DAY COME BACK MY WAY!!! It will come when God knows I need it the most, and it will usually

"If you have a need, sow a seed! Make sure it's the kind of seed you want to enjoy when it comes back your way."

come from unlikely sources. It has been said that if you help someone else fulfill their dream, God will send someone to help you fulfill yours. That is very true. So, when you look at the seeds you have planted in the past, are you seeing good fruit in your garden right now, or are you seeing a lot of weeds? That may have a lot to do with what you have been planting. Start today planting a seed of support, a seed of giving encouragement, a seed of patience, a seed of mercy, a financial seed, a seed of kind words, a seed of speaking positive about others instead of negative and watch what will happen! When you need nourishment in these areas, your garden will be ripe and plentiful in your time of need. What kind of day are you having? Maybe you need to plant a new seed! If you have a need, sow a seed! Make sure it's the kind of seed you want to enjoy when it comes back your way. And if you have a need, and you have sown good seeds, consider this word from God your return. Be encouraged friend. You don't see the results of a good garden overnight. Just know that the good seeds that you have sown are on their way!!!! God promised it, I didn't!

◆ ◆ ◆ ◆ ◆ ◆ ◆ ◆ ◆ ◆ ◆ ◆ ◆ ◆ ◆ ◆ ◆ ◆ ◆ ◆

Prayer

Dear Lord, forgive me of all the negative seeds I have sown. Help me today to sow some good seeds. Then give me the patience to wait on the great garden that will come up. Thank you Jesus. In Jesus' name I pray, Amen!

WEEK TWELVE

Get Your Business Straight!

Scripture

Proverbs 24:27 "Develop your business first before building your house."

◆ ◆ ◆ ◆ ◆ ◆ ◆ ◆ ◆ ◆ ◆ ◆ ◆ ◆ ◆ ◆ ◆ ◆ ◆

Things in life will go much smoother if we do them in the order God advises us to. One would think you would build a house before starting a business, but God says quite the opposite. He's not just talking about that business you have been dreaming of starting. No, He 's talking about your personal business. If you don't get your personal business straight before you get married, your house will never become a home. Handle up on those issues you haven't resolved. Get some of that debt down. Pay some of those bills. Get some insurance. Learn to cook. Learn to fix things around the house you're in. Learn a new trade. Try a new sport. Read a new book. Get in line with what God has for you to do. Many people I counsel who are now divorced, or having marital problems, usually always ran into problems because they didn't get the business of **selfishness** right before being in a relationship or mar-

◆ ◆ ◆ ◆ ◆

"If you get your business straight, it leaves room for you to add more to your life because you have a solid foundation."

◆ ◆ ◆ ◆ ◆

riage. You have to learn to share and compromise in relationships. You can't have everything you want. And if it is a business that you should develop, do it before getting in a committed relationship. Trying to start a big project such as a business or a new job while starting a relationship is not recommended by God or myself unless He specifically gives the go-ahead. Your attention will be divided, and someone or something will not get the attention it needs. So, timing is everything! Order is everything! Make sure you have one thing developed to the point where it can run smooth enough for you to start something else. Otherwise, you're making things stressful on yourself. Get your business straight, then start on that house. After all, if you don't have the money from the business, how will you pay for the house? Sip on that one for a while friend! If you get your business straight, it leaves room for you to add more to your life, because you have a solid foundation. What's your business? What your house? Get to working! There's a sea of blessings waiting on you!

◆ ◆ ◆ ◆ ◆ ◆ ◆ ◆ ◆ ◆ ◆ ◆ ◆ ◆ ◆ ◆ ◆ ◆ ◆ ◆

Prayer

Dear Lord, I ask that you show me areas in my life that need to be straightened out. Then help me make forward progress at your pace. In Jesus' name I pray, Amen.

WEEK THIRTEEN

Finish What You Started!

Scripture

Ecclesiastes 7:8 "Finishing is better than starting..."

◆◆◆◆◆◆◆◆◆◆◆◆◆◆◆◆◆◆◆◆

A few years ago, one of the best video games was made in "**Mortal Combat**." I myself have always loved video games and probably will never stop. I like challenging games. Mortal Combat is a gruesome, one-on-one fighting game that has many stages and people to defeat to complete the whole game. What I love the most about the game is that you can do a great job in starting a fight with your opponent, but during the fight you begin to lose energy. This happened to me several times. I started a fight off great, far ahead of my opponent, but did not totally defeat him before he began draining my energy to his level. I finally drained him to his last drop of energy. But the game trips out when the enemy gets to his last drop of energy. There is a voice that shouts to you while your enemy stands in a defeated stupor to "**FINISH HIM!** " Of course this is where you have to pull out your best, most creative move to totally destroy your enemy so he will not rise again. Do you

◆◆◆◆◆

"You have to keep fighting even though your strength, patience, and motivation has subsided."

◆◆◆◆◆

have anything you started well but then it began draining your energy so much so that you are struggling to complete it? Is it a diet, assignment, fast, relationship, job, book, degree, or even your life? My word to you today is "**Finish Him!**" You have to keep fighting even though your strength, patience, and motivation has subsided. You must complete what you started. If you don't, you won't be able to go to the next level of the game of life. Whatever your him is, "FINISH HIM!"

◆ ◆ ◆ ◆ ◆ ◆ ◆ ◆ ◆ ◆ ◆ ◆ ◆ ◆ ◆ ◆ ◆ ◆ ◆

Prayer

Dear Lord, give me the strength to complete the tasks that I have started. Give each person who reads this devotional grace to complete what the enemy is trying to defeat. With you, we can do all things. Begin giving us hope where we see no hope. Show us time where we see no time. Show us strategies that we have not seen before. If you want us to finish the things we have started, please do these things through us for your glory. You finished what you started early one Sunday morning. We want to be like you. In Jesus' name I pray, Amen.

WEEK FOURTEEN

Pay It Forward!

Scripture

2 Corinthians 1:4 "He comforts us in all of our troubles so that we can comfort others. When others are troubled, we will be able to give them the same comfort God has given us."

◆◆◆◆◆◆◆◆◆◆◆◆◆◆◆◆◆◆◆◆

There was a movie I was watching the other day about a little boy who did a good deed for this man whom it seemed life had given up on. The man asked him how he could pay him back. The little boy said, "Don't try to pay me back, **pay it forward.**" The whole movie was based on people not trying to pay people back, but to give to others what had been given to them. Isn't that what this scripture is saying? God has helped you in some way. How can you pay Him back and show your gratitude? You can never pay Him **back**, but you can show your gratitude by paying what He has done for you **forward**! Think of the things God has helped you with. Think of the lonely times when he sent someone into your life. Think of

◆◆◆◆◆

"..now that you realize how good He's been, what are you going to pay forward to show your gratitude not looking for anything in return?"

◆◆◆◆◆

the encouraging word He sent your way when you needed it. Sometimes it was a stranger who didn't even know you needed it, right? That was God's way of letting you know He still cares. So now that you realize how good He's been, what are you going to pay forward to show your gratitude not looking for anything in return? Do it today while it's on your mind. Someone needs something you have or your wisdom on how to handle a painful or difficult situation that God brought you through.

◆◆◆◆◆◆◆◆◆◆◆◆◆◆◆◆◆◆◆◆

Prayer

Dear Lord, reveal to me someone who needs me today. Use me to bless someone like you've blessed me. Then allow them to be a blessing to someone else. Thanks for all you've done. Help me show my gratitude by what I do and say the rest of this day. In Jesus' name I pray, Amen.

WEEK FIFTEEN

Don't Forget!

Scripture

Deuteronomy 6:12 "Beware lest you forget the Lord who brought you out of the land of Egypt, from the house of bondage."

◆ ◆ ◆ ◆ ◆ ◆ ◆ ◆ ◆ ◆ ◆ ◆ ◆ ◆ ◆ ◆ ◆ ◆ ◆ ◆

In the middle of getting a house ready to be painted it as part of an outreach effort to help those in the community near our church, it dawned on me that I had a grandfather whom I had not checked on to see if his house needed painting. You talk about convicting! I hadn't even called him in some time, and he only lives 38 miles away. So I went to see him two days later in the town I was born in, Terrell, Texas. My grandmother has been dead for about two years now after being married to him for almost 60 years. I guess it's uncomfortable for me to go there, because it's not the same without her. I still love him. I realized that while I was helping everybody else, I had forgotten about my own grandfather. Friend, sometimes we can be so godly in helping everybody else, encouraging everyone else, and forget about those closest to us. **I beg of you, don't forget where you come from.** You only have one

◆ ◆ ◆ ◆ ◆

"A true Christian loves the unlovely because they remember how they were when Christ found them."

◆ ◆ ◆ ◆ ◆

life to live, so make the most out of it. But make sure you give to those who made an investment in you, even those who can't do anything for you. They're still family. I also saw one of my uncles who is known as one of the drunks in the town. I saw him and picked him up in my truck that God had blessed me with and went for a ride with him. I hugged him, because he is my uncle no matter what he smells like or looks like. **Never be ashamed of your family.** If it wasn't for the grace of God, where would you be? Start today thanking God for what He has done in the past, and for what He's going to do on a higher level in the future. **Don't forget where you came from! A true Christian loves the unlovely, because they remember how they were when Christ found them. How is your LOVE LIFE lately?**

◆ ◆ ◆ ◆ ◆ ◆ ◆ ◆ ◆ ◆ ◆ ◆ ◆ ◆ ◆ ◆ ◆ ◆ ◆

Prayer

Dear Lord, show me where I may think I am too important. Show me where I am not loving like you. Show me where my priorities are messed up. I ask that you forgive me when I recognize my flaws. Then give me the wisdom and strength to correct where I strayed. Thank you Jesus for loving me in spite of me. Help me show others **True** and **Real Love.** In Jesus name, Amen.

WEEK SIXTEEN

Can You Hear Me Now?

Scripture

Jonah (1:17;2:1) Now the Lord had arranged a great fish to swallow Jonah. And Jonah was inside the fish for three days and three nights. Then Jonah prayed to the Lord his God from inside the fish.

◆ ◆ ◆ ◆ ◆ ◆ ◆ ◆ ◆ ◆ ◆ ◆ ◆ ◆ ◆ ◆ ◆ ◆ ◆ ◆

One of my favorite commercials is the Verizon Cell Phone commercial where the man is standing in the middle of a football field and simply says to the person on the other line "Can you hear me now?" Before he moves from that spot, he waits for a response on the other end. When it seems he gets the right response, he simply says "Good" and moves on to the next area. God had to use this same method with Jonah. Apparently when God told Jonah to do something he didn't want to do, Jonah didn't hear God clear and didn't really believe God meant what He said. So God had to allow a great fish to swallow Jonah up for three days, because he had gone in the opposite direction of where God told him to go. Now I can just hear God asking

◆ ◆ ◆ ◆ ◆

"Are you having a hard time because of disobedience? Can You Hear God Now? Good! Maybe you can move to the next level now."

◆ ◆ ◆ ◆ ◆

Jonah, "Can You Hear Me Now?" I guess the answer must have been, “Yes” from Jonah, because he began praying inside of the fish. Then I hear God saying, "**Good**" and allowing the fish to spit Jonah up on the shore. Has God been telling you he wants you to forgive someone, help someone, leave something behind, or move forward in some way? I advise you to accept His will and do it before you find yourself in Jonah's shoes. It may be a whale of finances, guilt, frustration, pain etc... Are you having a hard time because of disobedience? **Can You Hear God Now**? Good! Maybe you can move to the next level now. He only wants what's best for you.

◆◆◆◆◆◆◆◆◆◆◆◆◆◆◆◆◆◆◆

Prayer

Dear Lord, whatever you have for me to do, please give me the strength to do it. I want to hear you clearly even if it is something I really don't want to do. Please forgive me for not moving when you want me to move. I just want to be in your will at all cost. I love you. In Jesus' name I pray, Amen.

WEEK SEVENTEEN

Barber Shop

Scripture

Judges 16:19 "Delilah lulled Samson to sleep with his head in her lap, and she called in a man to shave off his hair, making his capture certain. And his strength left him"

◆◆◆◆◆◆◆◆◆◆◆◆◆◆◆◆◆◆◆◆

There's nothing like having a fresh cut or a fresh perm is it? You go to the salon of a person you trust, lay your head back for a wash or sit up straight and let them tie this thing around your neck for a cut. Over the years I've found that you can't let everybody touch your head. Some people do not know what they are doing. They may look like they know, because they are in the right place. You assume they have a license. You assume they have skills, because they have the look. If their shop is noted for having a great reputation for great hairstyles, it makes you go to that shop doesn't it? Well, Samson saw someone he didn't trust with his head at first. He went to her thinking he was at a hotel but began to share too much, fell asleep, and woke up and recognized he was at **the barber shop**! Have you ever walked into something thinking it was one way, only to realize that you got comfortable, closed your eyes because you trusted the people or person in that place, and when you came to, you recognized things weren't what they seemed before you let go of your trust? Samson got his

◆◆◆◆◆

"Don't lose your strength or your vision for your life fooling around with a bootleg barber!"

◆◆◆◆◆

hair cut, lost his strength and his vision, because he played around with something he should not have. He woke up with a fresh cut that he had to pay for with his very life and had a new style he didn't want. Have you been deceived friend? Be careful who you let touch those important areas in your life. They may look like they know what they're doing, but check out some of their clients. If everyone else they have dealt with has been messed up, didn't like the service, never would refer anyone to them, then chances are you may need to do business elsewhere before you become a victim. Delilah was no barber. She called a man in to cut off Samson's hair. The devil will make people plot together to take you out. Be careful whom you trust. Don't be afraid to trust people, just be cautious. They may want something more from you than you think! Who or what is messing with your head today? Make sure you walk away looking better than when you came in, or you may need to go elsewhere. Don't lose your strength or your vision for your life fooling around with a bootleg barber! Find someone you can trust with your life and your head. You don't want to walk around looking crazy do you? And on that note, in the words of Cedric The Entertainer "I'll Holla!"

◆◆◆◆◆◆◆◆◆◆◆◆◆◆◆◆◆◆◆◆

Prayer

Dear Lord, help me know where to lay my head. Help me know who to trust. Bring people into my life that are experienced in the areas I need help in. Thank you Lord. I know you want me to look nice and not feel confused or unloved, because I have been letting my head fall into the wrong hands. In Jesus name I pray, amen.

WEEK EIGHTEEN

Wrong Time, Wrong Place

Scripture

Jeremiah 16:1-2 Then the word of the Lord came to me and said, "You must not marry and have sons and daughters in this place."

◆◆◆◆◆◆◆◆◆◆◆◆◆◆◆◆◆◆◆◆

Have you ever wanted to do something but just didn't know if it was time or not? Have your ever made a decision and had regrets after making it? Friend, your life is very important to God. Sometimes He has to allow us to hurt in order to stop us from making a long term commitment to something because we figured it was the right choice to make. God told Jeremiah that He could not get married at this time in his life, nor in the place he wanted to live. Think of that. Why? God told him in the next few verses that his children and he would suffer because God was doing something with that place. Jeremiah could only see the now and not the future. He had a vision of what his future would look like, but God knew what his future there really would have been like if he would have made that

◆◆◆◆◆

"Even if it hurts, wipe your tears and move forward. There's something bigger waiting on you!"

◆◆◆◆◆

choice. Don't be guilty of choosing the wrong thing at the wrong time. Whatever choice you make, make sure it is God who is telling you to make it, and make his choice. He may tell you to drop everything you know to be familiar. He may tell you to move to another city, leave a relationship, or a job. If you don't leave voluntarily, He may have to boot you out for your own good. That thing you want may look good right now, but it may be going down in a short period of time. Don't get caught on the Titanic. Move when God says move. Choose what God says choose. Even if it hurts, wipe your tears and move forward. There's something bigger waiting on you!

Prayer

◆◆◆◆◆◆◆◆◆◆◆◆◆◆◆◆◆◆◆◆

Dear Lord, please help me to hear your voice over my emotions. Lead me by your Spirit. I just want to be in your will, even if it hurts. In Jesus' name, amen.

WEEK NINETEEN

Is Your Pride More Important Than Your Progress?

Scripture

Matthew 18:3 "I assure you, unless you turn from your sins and become as little children, you will never get into the Kingdom of Heaven."

◆ ◆ ◆ ◆ ◆ ◆ ◆ ◆ ◆ ◆ ◆ ◆ ◆ ◆ ◆ ◆ ◆ ◆ ◆ ◆

Pride is something that robs us of the very benefits that God has in store for us. What is pride? Pride is you being stubborn and not yielding to God because you want your way, or because you think it will make you feel and look better! You can be wrong and know you're wrong, but Pride will make you stay wrong because you don't want to look like a failure in front of people. What is pride? Pride is a bowl full of foolishness. Pride will keep you from taking any job when you have been laid off, because you won't work unless you get what you think you are worth. All the while, you have bills piling up, creditors calling, and you are still trying to live a lifestyle that you can no longer afford right now. Then, you have the audacity to blame God for this when there are other jobs that will help you make it until you get your next break. Jesus was saying that unless we become like children in His sight, we will not enter the Kingdom of God. Children know that they are dependent, not independent. Children ask when they need help. Children forgive easily. Children play together after they have a disagreement. The Kingdom of God is not just Heaven. It is the better life that He promised us in John 10:10 right here on earth. Understand friend, if you have been a giver, God is answering

◆ ◆ ◆ ◆ ◆

"I promise you if you get rid of your pride He'll blow your mind."

◆ ◆ ◆ ◆ ◆

your prayer when you ask Him for something by sending people your way who will give back to you. Have you been turning the answers to your prayers away because of Pride? You don't want people in your business, right? They will really be in your business if you don't do something now won't they? Save yourself some extra heartache. Why pray to God if you only want Him to answer your way? He has millions of ways to get you what you need. "If you're faithful over a few things He'll make you ruler over many." Maybe your being laid off is a test. Maybe God wants to see if you'll make due with what you have and realize who you are whether you work at McDonald's or Motorola. Or, can you see your value through that thick cloud of Pride? Don't spend time feeling sorry for yourself. Learn to make adjustments, smile, and say to yourself "I'll Be Back. In the meantime, I have to pass this test!" Friend, when that gas hand gets low, the groceries get low, remember that God ain't low. I promise you if you get rid of your pride He'll blow your mind. There is a difference between asking and begging. Pray about who to ask. God won't lead you wrong. "Ask and it shall be given. Seek and ye shall find..." Ask God first. He'll show you what to do. Everything you need is right at your fingertips. Everything. You just have to let go of that pride, ask God to reveal to you His resources, and enjoy your day!

◆ ◆ ◆ ◆ ◆ ◆ ◆ ◆ ◆ ◆ ◆ ◆ ◆ ◆ ◆ ◆ ◆ ◆ ◆

Prayer

Lord, please show me where my pride is hindering you giving me what I need. Show me the difference between what I want and what I need. Then, help me do what I need to do in order to get the things I want. Thanks for helping me with my pride. In Jesus' name I pray, amen.

WEEK TWENTY

Run Tel Dat!

Scripture

Luke 7:22 Then Jesus answered, "Go and tell John the things you have SEEN and heard: that the blind see, the lame walk, the lepers are cured, the deaf hear, the dead are raised to life, and the Good News is being preached to the poor. And tell him "God blesses those who are not offended by me."

◆◆◆◆◆◆◆◆◆◆◆◆◆◆◆◆◆◆◆◆

I know many of you have seen Martin Lawrence's new movie Runteldat. For those who are ebonically challenged, (Run Tell That). It is about what the real deal is in his life from his point of view-Straight from the horses mouth. Well, Jesus is being questioned by some disciples as to whether or not He is who He says He is. He didn't answer by trying to explain who He was. He answered by pointing to what He had accomplished. What He accomplished was the job description of the person they were looking for, "The Savior of the World." He was saying, "Run and tell John the Baptist, while he is in jail doubting who I am after being with me, that my works match my words." Friend, you don't have to spin your wheels trying to prove yourself by talking. **Just show up**. People will know who you are by the time you leave their presence. They won't be so impressed by what YOU said you could do, but by what you actually did.

◆◆◆◆◆

"Usually your critics give you Free Press to make everyone want to know more about you. "

◆◆◆◆◆

Then they will RUNTELDAT. Who are you based on what you do? If you know who you are, don't worry about what others may say about you. Usually your critics give you Free Press to make everyone want to know more about you. And when the people they told erroneous things to about you come to see you, those people will RUNTELDAT you are better than what was said and they will become a part of your support team. Actions do speak louder than words. Jesus is the bomb, and He has proven that time and time again. He is the only way to heaven. He is all you will ever need. The next time someone tries to bring you gossip, tell them about Jesus and say, "**RUNTELDAT to somebody**!" They just may lead someone to Christ by doing so.

◆ ◆ ◆ ◆ ◆ ◆ ◆ ◆ ◆ ◆ ◆ ◆ ◆ ◆ ◆ ◆ ◆ ◆ ◆

Prayer

Lord, thank you for all those who are reading this devotional. I pray that you help all of us follow your example and be who you want us to be even when we are questioned by others in our lives. Help us not retaliate when ignorant things are done to us and vicious lies are spread on us. Let us understand that people wouldn't know us if nothing was said about us and that all things eventually work for the good. I pray that more of us RUNTEL the goodness of who you are and what you have done; of what you are doing, and what you can do for ourselves and others. I love you Jesus. In Jesus name I pray, Amen.

WEEK TWENTY-ONE

Wait a Minute!

Scripture

Romans 8:24-25 "For if you already have something, you don't need to hope for it. But if we look forward to something we don't have yet, we must wait patiently and confidently."

◆ ◆ ◆ ◆ ◆ ◆ ◆ ◆ ◆ ◆ ◆ ◆ ◆ ◆ ◆ ◆ ◆ ◆ ◆ ◆

Watching a mother talk with her child as the child keeps asking the mother for another bite of some delicious chocolate cake, the mother gives the child another bite and continues to do another task while feeding the child. The mother is balancing her checkbook and feeding her child at the same time. The child only focuses on the cake that he can **see** and **understand** and hopes for another piece. The mother trying to balance her checkbook and feeling rushed as the child cries for her attention for more cake, simply looks at the child and says those famous words "**Wait A Minute!**" The child is so focused on the cake, hoping for another helping of it that he gets impatient. He doesn't even realize that if the checkbook isn't balanced correctly he may not even have a roof over its head. He is so focused on the cake and gets upset when he can't have another piece to satisfy his hunger. He doesn't understand that the cake is coming and there is another plan the parent is work-

◆ ◆ ◆ ◆ ◆

"Wait A Minute, Wait Patiently, and have the Confidence that God loves you and knows exactly what you need and want."

◆ ◆ ◆ ◆ ◆

ing on that will last long after the cake is gone. Friend, what cake are you wanting but seem to not be able to have right now? Is it a cake job, relationship, home, money, car, peace of mind? Listen, God is working on something in another area of your life that is bigger than what you are **wanting** or **seeing** right now. The cake is still in His hands, and you will get it. Just let Him balance the books of your life and the cake will taste much better when you get it because you'll know that that's not the last piece you'll ever get. You're focused on a piece of cake and **God is trying to get you to own a bakery.** You'll get your cake if you'll just "**Wait A Minute**, **Wait Patiently**, and **have the Confidence** that God loves you and knows exactly what you need and want." Do you want that cake? Then Wait A Minute. How long is a minute? You'll forget how long once your cake arrives. I promise you that the time you waited won't matter. Be patient friend.

◆ ◆ ◆ ◆ ◆ ◆ ◆ ◆ ◆ ◆ ◆ ◆ ◆ ◆ ◆ ◆ ◆ ◆ ◆

Prayer

Oh Lord, thanks for reminding me that you are in control. Thanks for reminding me that you love me enough to delay one thing, because you're working on a larger scale that I can't see. Help me to wait patiently with expectation and hope for the things I have already prayed for. I love you Jesus. In Jesus' name I pray, Amen.

WEEK TWENTY-TWO

Four Reasons to Smile!

Scripture

Genesis 12:2-3 "I will make you into a great nation and I will bless you; I will make your name great, and you will be a blessing. I will bless those who bless you and whoever curses you I will curse"

Hey friend, did you know that if you are a child of God you are so blessed that it will spill over to other people? I guess you don't know what blessed means, huh? Blessed means that you have favor with God. It means you are His favor-ite child. He loves all of His children and all are His favorites. Abraham was a child of God, and we are descendants of Abraham if we are Christians. Look at the three reasons we have to smile.

"Every time you feel the blessings have stopped... Wham!!! Another blessing!!!"

(1) **I will bless you** (The word for bless means I will continue to bless you. Every time you feel the blessings have stopped... Wham!!! Another blessing!!! Stop looking for people to bless you. God already has you taken care of.

(2) **I will make your name great (**Are you trying to promote your name yourself? God says, relax. At the right time I will tell everyone about your business, your good qualities, everything good that people need to

know. Let God promote you. When He does It, it always lasts. It also cost less.

(3) **You will be a blessing (**God says, you won't just have "enough", but you'll have leftovers to share with other people. Remember, when you get it, God wants you to share it!

(4) **I will bless those who bless you and curse those who curse you** (Anybody who treats you well will be blessed by God for doing so! Why? Because you are special to God. Tell those who you know "Man, you better be good to me so God can hook you up!" Also, He will curse those who curse you. He will take care of those who do you wrong. God has your back either way!

Listen friend, there is no need to be depressed. You are blessed and will be blessed in the future. I didn't promise it, God did! So why is it difficult for you right now? The devil doesn't want you to know the truth. Well, I'm telling you the secret he's trying to hide from you. Raise up your hands and say, **"I'M A BLESSED CHILD OF GOD CAUSE' MY DADDY LOVES ME! DADDY LOVES THE KIDS!!!"**

◆ ◆ ◆ ◆ ◆ ◆ ◆ ◆ ◆ ◆ ◆ ◆ ◆ ◆ ◆ ◆ ◆ ◆ ◆

Prayer

God, help me to believe what you just told me. In Jesus' name I pray, amen!

WEEK TWENTY-THREE

I SEE DEAD PEOPLE!

Scripture

Exodus 14:30 "And the Israelites could see the bodies of the Egyptians washed up on shore."

◆ ◆ ◆ ◆ ◆ ◆ ◆ ◆ ◆ ◆ ◆ ◆ ◆ ◆ ◆ ◆ ◆ ◆ ◆ ◆

You know this familiar story don't you? Moses and the children of Israel cross the Red Sea, right? Well, after they cross over, they get to look back at what God had rescued them from...the floating bodies of what was causing them stress. Friend, have you ever had the opportunity to pay off some bill collectors, or pull out a newly printed credit report. Those lines marked **paid** are "**Dead People.**" Have you ever had a relationship that God graciously brought you through and you now see them either alone or with someone else and you don't want them anymore? Those are "**Dead People**!" I know you can find something today to look back at and see that it is powerless to control you anymore in your life. It is not able to control your thought process. Maybe it was something you really wanted but God wouldn't give it to you. Those are "**Dead People!**" Dead people equal dead issues. Stop

◆ ◆ ◆ ◆ ◆

"Dead people equal dead issues. Stop letting something that is over keep coming alive. "

◆ ◆ ◆ ◆ ◆

letting something that is over keep coming alive. Look back at it and say, "While you lay there powerless, I want to thank you for helping me be what I am today. Thank you for helping me learn to pray and get closer to God." Then say, "But you should have killed me and made me give up while you had the chance. So now I must quote those great words of a well known role model of mine, the Road Runner.....Beep Beep!!! " Don't play with dead people or dead things. There's something wrong with you if you do.

◆ ◆ ◆ ◆ ◆ ◆ ◆ ◆ ◆ ◆ ◆ ◆ ◆ ◆ ◆ ◆ ◆ ◆ ◆ ◆

Prayer

Dear Lord, thank you for allowing me to look behind me and see things that you kept me from and brought me out of. Seeing where I've come from gives me hope of where I can go. If you brought me from all of those floating bodies and issues, surely it was for a greater purpose for my future. I'm excited Lord about what you're about to do in me. In Jesus' name I pray. Amen.

WEEK TWENTY-FOUR

Are you down with OPP?

Scripture

Exodus 1:12 The more the Egyptians oppressed them, the more quickly the Israelites multiplied.

Picture the scene. The Egyptians who are mean, cruel, and using the Israelites for their own agenda, are steadily trying to make life harder for them. They give them more work with less strategies to help them be successful. They give them more hours with less help and less pay. Ever been there?

"Every time they throw things your way, fix them and send them back in better condition."

The ruler of the Egyptians felt threatened by the education, wisdom, and intelligence of the Israelites, so they were insecure. Insecure people usually try to make your life more difficult, because you are a threat to them. You may look better, smell better, and feel better about yourself, so to bring you to their level, they will try to make you feel oppressed or depressed. You did see the first 3 letters of oppressed didn't you? **O.P.P.** Insecure people have their **O**wn **P**ersonal **P**roblems. Don't let their personal problems become yours. Use what they are trying to use against you for good. Every time they throw things your way, fix them and send them back in better condition. Every time they send you lemons, take the seeds out, put them in the ground, grow you some lemon trees and start a business. Face it friend, some people are just not going to like you! Get over it! But I did ask are you down with OPP? I am. You know what it stands for to me? **O**verlooking **P**itiful **P**eople! You see friend, some people you don't even need to waste your time on. They hinder your growth when you spend too much energy on them. Don't try to fight every battle. Choose which ones you will fight. Overlook them and pray for them. Jesus did. He was on the cross and said, "Forgive them for they know not what they do!" Those people didn't even know that while they were tearing him down, they were preparing him to be lifted up to a level even higher than they could imagine. You down with OPP? Yeah, you know me! Think about it!

◆ ◆ ◆ ◆ ◆ ◆ ◆ ◆ ◆ ◆ ◆ ◆ ◆ ◆ ◆ ◆ ◆ ◆ ◆

Prayer

Thank you Jesus for deliverance from people! Help me be what you want me to be. Bless my enemies. Forgive them, for they know not what they do. For those who have problems with their bosses, give them strength. For those who have problems with relationships, give them strength. For those who have problems with family members, give them strength. For anyone who is dealing with Other People's Problems, give them wisdom in Overlooking Pitiful People and praying for them. In Jesus name I pray, Amen.

WEEK TWENTY-FIVE

Die Another Day

Scripture

Philippians 4:13 "For I can do everything with the help of Christ who gives me strength."

Have you ever had one of those mornings where you were not feeling like you wanted to get out of bed? You began thinking of what you had to do, and you really didn't feel like dealing with it that day? I had one this morning. And let me tell you, I almost didn't get up. It's cold outside; it's the holiday season; I want to be on vacation on some warm island, **but I had work to do**. Well, as hard as it was, the thought came to me that I have come too far, and God has been too good for me to complain about what I had to do. He began to remind me of what needed to be done and the sacrifice it would take for it to get done on my part. Beware when laziness, being tired, frustration, and comfort try to cause you to waste a day that need not be wasted. There is a time for rest, but today wasn't one of them. The devil was trying to put me behind schedule so he could kill my peace and my future. You have a choice of getting up or laying there and letting what you're trying

"When you don't go places because of what you know you will have to deal with but you really need to go..."

to build as well as yourself in a sense DIE. When you lay in your depression you, die that day. When you are lazy, you die that day. When you don't go places because of what you know you will have to deal with, but you really need to go, you die that day. Death is being unfruitful. This verse came to mind, "I can do all things through Christ who gives me strength!" You know what, I really can. You really can. There is truth in God's word. I said that aloud, and I now am having a lovely day. Tell the devil or your attitudes or feelings, "I'm going to die another day, but this ain't the one. Life is too short and my purpose is too great for me to die today!" **Live Friend! Press through it.** You have so much ahead of you to stop now!

◆◆◆◆◆◆◆◆◆◆◆◆◆◆◆◆◆◆◆◆

Prayer:

Dear Lord, thank you for having a job, life, sight, hearing, a class to go to, a car to drive, a place to live. The very fact that I have phone bills and electric bills is a sign that I have a roof over my head. I thank you that I shall not die, but live because you are my life and my strength. Bless every person who reads this devotional to press through every attack of the enemy on their progress. Thank you for comfort in loneliness, financial difficulty, and every other situation that makes them feel like they are dying. Bring them back to life the way you want them to live! In Jesus' name I pray, amen!

WEEK TWENTY-SIX

You Belong There!

Scripture

Luke 4:18 "The Spirit of the Lord is on me because He has anointed me to preach good news to the poor, to proclaim freedom for the prisoners and recovery of sight for the blind and release the oppressed."

◆◆◆◆◆◆◆◆◆◆◆◆◆◆◆◆◆◆◆◆

Friend, why are you here on this earth? Why do you work where you work? Why are you married to whom you're married to? Why do you spend time doing what you do? Could it be that God has given you special ability to handle what you do? **Of course!!!** Jesus knew why He came to the earth. It is listed in the verse above. He would not let anything...a backstabbing Judas, being born in a terrible environment, church people that didn't like him, people not understanding Him, people not believing in who He was, or His closest companions leaving Him to die alone on a cross stop Him from doing what He knew He was placed on this earth to do! Are you having problems in your marriage? Are you having problems in your family? Are you having problems in your career? Are you having problems with your own life in any area? Listen friend, don't ever get to the point where you feel **power-**

◆◆◆◆◆

"Remember whose you are and put a kool-aid grin on your face and get to stepping!!!"

◆◆◆◆◆

less. You are **never** powerless. When you feel that way, you just need to ask God to show you what power you do have. You are a Christian, the sibling of Jesus Christ and the Son of God Almighty and you tell me you are powerless? **Nonsense!** Get on your knees and ask Him to show you what you can do in the situation, then do it! Remember, the Red Sea was a Dead End until Moses talked to God. What's your Red Sea situation? Stretch out your prayer life and get ready for another realm of victory you never would have known had you not been where you are! **Don't stop, stretch!** Remember whose you are and put a kool-aid grin on your face and get to stepping!!! **You belong where you are,** so stop looking for something better. Make where you are better. There is another way....find it. This time you can't run. Stand and be strong!

◆ ◆ ◆ ◆ ◆ ◆ ◆ ◆ ◆ ◆ ◆ ◆ ◆ ◆ ◆ ◆ ◆ ◆ ◆

Prayer

Dear Jesus, help those who read this to see the value of where they are in life right now. Help them to know that you have a reason for them being where they are, and it is for their good in the end. Help them and myself to submit to your will and not run from what makes us uncomfortable. We just want your will no matter what. In Jesus' name I pray, amen.

WEEK TWENTY-SEVEN

Who's Your DJ?

Scripture

Luke 7:32 (b): "We played the flute for you, and you did not dance; we sang a dirge, and you did not cry."

You know this scene don't you brothers? You're at a party and you see someone you want to dance with. They are hanging with some friends, or they may be all alone on the wall. You walk over to her and ask her to dance. If she told you no, the excuse would be what? **The DJ is not playing my song!** Listen friend, you have a choice to dance to whatever music in life that you choose. So it is with other choices you have to make in life. Is there someone or some situation trying to make you dance to its beat? Some people get frustrated when they can't control or manipulate you. How so? They play the song of sarcasm and you don't dance. They play the song of not speaking to you and you don't dance. They play the song of not including you and you don't dance. They play the song of a guilt trip and you don't dance. They play the song of they can't help

"You can't hear that? The Lord is playing a song of peace, and that's my jam!"

you and you don't dance and get disturbed by it. Afterwards they walk away and you begin dancing and smiling? When they look at you in confusion, look at them and say "You can't hear that? The Lord is playing a song of peace, and that's my jam!" Don't dance until **DJ G.O.D** hits the turntables from heaven. Always keep a song in your heart. Then you won't dance to the beat of those you don't want to dance with! Get your Holy Ghost groove on baby! **God's playing your song.** Put a smile on your face and listen to the music! What DJ's are trying to play music in your life? Tell them, "**That ain't my song!"**

◆◆◆◆◆◆◆◆◆◆◆◆◆◆◆◆◆◆◆◆

Prayer

Dear Lord, thank you for giving me peace in the midst of a challenging and changing world. I love the music you play. It's like **smooth jazz** when the devil is trying to make me **rock and roll**. I love you Jesus. In Jesus' name I pray, amen.

WEEK TWENTY-EIGHT

Help from the Spirit

Scripture

Romans 8:26 "Likewise the Spirit also helps in our weaknesses. For we do not know what we should pray for as we ought, but the Spirit Himself makes intercession for us with groanings which cannot be uttered."

◆ ◆ ◆ ◆ ◆ ◆ ◆ ◆ ◆ ◆ ◆ ◆ ◆ ◆ ◆ ◆ ◆ ◆ ◆ ◆

Have you ever tried to pray but just didn't know what to say? Have you ever known you needed to pray but you didn't want to sound dumb coming before God? Have you ever had a situation that was hard to pray for? Have you ever been hurting so bad that you couldn't even open your mouth? God knows that even the best of us don't know exactly how to pray. That's why He allows Himself (The Holy Spirit) to pray for us. What's actually going on in prayer is God is talking to Himself from your heart. God is in you analyzing the situation. Your mind is thinking you need one thing so you pray for something. The Holy Spirit knows there is another thing behind what you see, so he takes what you have said and makes it correct before it reaches Heaven. When it reaches Heaven Jesus gets it and says, "Daddy this is what your child needs." That's called intercession. You may not get it out right, but get it out of your mouth. And when you can't get it out because you don't have the strength, He can interpret that too.

◆ ◆ ◆ ◆ ◆

"And when you can't get it out because you don't have the strength..."

◆ ◆ ◆ ◆ ◆

God hears us when we pray with a pure heart. We pray better when we know His word better. When you know His Word better, you'll learn more of what to ask for and what not to ask for. But pray now based on what you do know. And as you grow, your prayer life will grow. But remember, we always need the Holy Spirit because He is the one who helps us pray more effectively. Before you pray, ask God to forgive you of your sins. This ensures you of no hindrances to your prayer. Then ask the Holy Spirit to lead you as to how you should pray. Then begin praying. Your prayer life will be more effective if you let the expert pray through you.... The Holy Spirit. He's never had an unanswered prayer! Why? He's God too! Now go pray about that situation and believe that God will respond to your prayer. And believe that it will Work together for your Good!

◆◆◆◆◆◆◆◆◆◆◆◆◆◆◆◆◆◆◆

Prayer

Dear Jesus, please forgive me of any sins I've committed this day. Holy Spirit, pray through me so I can pray in God's Will. Dear Lord, bless every person who is reading this. If they are not saved, convict them and show them your love. If they are hurting, comfort them with your arms of love. If they need direction show them the way that they should go. If they need financial assistance give them the job, wisdom or position they need to be successful for you. Thank you for answering my prayer. In Jesus name I pray, Amen.

WEEK TWENTY-NINE

Leaving the Right Way!

Scripture

Philippians (1:23-24) "I'm torn between two desires: Sometimes I want to live, and sometimes I long to go be with Christ. That would be far better for me, but it is better for you that I live."

◆◆◆◆◆◆◆◆◆◆◆◆◆◆◆◆◆◆◆◆

Have you ever been in a situation where you really wanted to leave because things did not seem to be in your favor? Have you ever been on a job where it seemed that you weren't growing? Have you ever been in a relationship where it seemed that you were not getting all out of it that you needed? Listen friend, we all face situations where it seems we've done all we could do there. We've all faced situations where we know there was something better ahead for us and it would be easy for us to just leave to go ahead and move on with our lives. The one thing we have to be cautious of is that we do not become selfish and think more about OUR comfort than the blessings or the struggles we could put on others if we left because "WE" were no longer comfortable. I once was a supervisor at UPS, and I loved the money, the people, and everything else. I knew that's not what I wanted to do the rest of my life, so I began searching for another job. My time there was up. Even though I knew my time was coming to a close, I had to realize that I shouldn't move too fast. You see, there were peo-

◆◆◆◆◆

"The way you leave one situation is the way you enter a new situation."

◆◆◆◆◆

ple who depended on me. There were people who would never know Jesus if I hadn't stayed a little longer. God has a purpose for you wherever He places you. Your workplace, your church and everything your involved in has a purpose in your life. You serve a purpose. Some people are being blessed by your presence, and you don't even realize it. You may never know until after you leave. Look around the place you are trying to leave. Before you go, ask yourself these questions. "Am I leaving with the right attitude?" "When I leave, will people respect me even though they don't like me, because I finished well?" It may be your time to leave, but God is holding you up because He wants you to see how valuable you are while you are there. Understand this: The way you leave one situation is the way you enter a new situation. Leave with a good work ethic. Leave with a good attitude. And when it's time to go, God will give you peace because you have finished everything you were supposed to in that season of your life. Just because the door is open to leave doesn't mean you're close to the exit. But, you are on your way. Before you walk away, make sure you cross-over with
class!

◆◆◆◆◆◆◆◆◆◆◆◆◆◆◆◆◆◆◆

Prayer

Dear Lord, thank you for where I am in life. I ask that you not let me leave this place until I have done all, learned all, and helped all the people that you wanted me to. When my time is up, I'll give you praise and go into my next adventure with the same attitude. In Jesus' name I pray, amen.

WEEK THIRTY

What Are Your Focused On?

Scripture

Philippians 4:8 "Fix your thoughts on what is true an honorable and right. Think about things that are pure and lovely and admirable. Think about things that are excellent and worthy of praise."

◆◆◆◆◆◆◆◆◆◆◆◆◆◆◆◆◆◆◆◆

In the book, Five Star Church, a statement was made saying, "*That which holds your attention determines one's actions.*" Friend, what has your attention? Whatever you focus on is taking up valuable time and energy. Is what you are focused on worth the energy and time you're giving it? If you focus on the negative, and see only the negative, do you feel that you will have a positive attitude? If you focus on what people think about your performance at work, home, your clothing, or friends, you will either end up upset or trying to change to make others feel comfortable with who you are. Is that worth your focus? I think that just may take too much work. So what should you focus on? God is not telling us not to be in the state of denial and act as if there is no problem. He is telling us to recognize the problems we have, but focus on what He can do about it. What do you see in your situation? There were twins who were being tested on their

◆◆◆◆◆

"We have a choice of what we will focus on. Even the things that are right in our face."

◆◆◆◆◆

attitude. One had a negative attitude, the other a positive one. They both were given a present. In the present was a bowl of horse manure. The negative twin said no one loved her. She began to complain and murmur. The positive twin opened her box and began to smile. She said, "With this much manure there must be a pony somewhere that someone is trying to give me!" So she began looking around and sure enough there were two ponies outside. There has to be some good in it somewhere! We have a choice of what we will focus on; even the things that are right in our face. We must choose to focus on what will help us have the right attitude. Situations are always going to come into our lives whether good or bad. Since we know that, we can be prepared before they come by keeping our focus on positive things. Negative people help you focus on negative things from their negative viewpoint. Positive people see the positive even in the negative situation. Which one are you? If you're negative, you have the formula in today's verse to change that.

◆ ◆ ◆ ◆ ◆ ◆ ◆ ◆ ◆ ◆ ◆ ◆ ◆ ◆ ◆ ◆ ◆ ◆ ◆

Prayer

Dear Lord, help me see the good in every situation. Help me see the good in people. My attitude should be positive, so help me focus on positive things in the midst of negative situations. I need my joy and peace so help me with this please. Thanks in advance for answering this prayer Jesus. In Jesus' name, amen.

WEEK THIRTY-ONE

The Secret to being Strong

Scripture

2 Corinthians 12:9 "'My gracious favor is all you need. My power works best in your weakness."

◆◆◆◆◆◆◆◆◆◆◆◆◆◆◆◆◆◆◆◆

How strong are you? Are you strong enough to handle anything? I mean anything. I'm not. I am learning everyday that I am not as strong as I thought I was. The closer you get to Christ, the more you begin to realize that all of the situations: death of friends, death of loved ones, loss of jobs, etc... should all make you lose your mind. The reality is, God gives you strength in those times to handle all of them. You know what I'm saying? Like the times when you felt weak in your stomach. Like the time you didn't want to face people but went to work anyway. Like the time you didn't think you could see them again without getting mad or upset but you made it through it. You see, we turn to God when pain hits our lives. That is the only way we survive. What about the times that you didn't turn to God? What about the people who don't even know God and they make it through these same situations? You see friend, God doesn't just give strength to those who ask. He gives strength to those who need it, sometimes even when they don't feel they de-

◆◆◆◆◆

"God has some strength in reserve for you. He knew you would need it today."

◆◆◆◆◆

serve to ask. If you are not saved and are making it through, that's because God's grace of strength is working for you. It's not luck. He's keeping you together, unsaved, long enough so you could have time to get to know your true source of power in Jesus Christ. If you are saved and don't call on Him, He can choose to hook you up, too. What is the meaning of all of this then? Here's the point. Don't wait to get in trouble to depend on God. Don't just depend on Him when everything is going wrong. He can make you stronger when you feel strong and make you strong when you feel weak. So what's the secret of being strong? Staying dependent on the true source of strength every single day. Of course I'm talking about spending time in prayer to Jesus and being obedient to what He says. Are you having a difficult time right now and almost feel like giving up? You're weak right now. That's okay. God has some strength in reserve for you. He knew you would need it today. Just ask Him to be there with you in it, and you'll make it through. That's a promise. Try it and see. I dare you!

◆◆◆◆◆◆◆◆◆◆◆◆◆◆◆◆◆◆◆

Prayer

Dear Lord, thank you for being so strong for me and in me. You have always been there for me. Help me to depend on you more and more everyday. I cannot even depend on myself 100%. I know I can trust you because you can always be consistent and loving, and caring to me in any stage of my life. Be strong in my weakness. Thanks for the extra strength that I need. In Jesus' name I pray, amen.

WEEK THIRTY-TWO

Put the Word on It!

Scripture

Isaiah 55:11 "So shall My word be that goes forth from My mouth; It shall not return to Me void, But it shall accomplish what I please, And it shall prosper in the thing for which I sent it."

Your prayers will have more power, and will mean more to you and God when we pray the Word of God into our situation. Listen; God wrote the Bible right? We do call it "The Word of God" right? Can He deny what He says if He said it? No! He said He does not lie. We must get to know His Word and what it means so we can tell Him what He said about us and our situation. You do know that there is a Word for your situation don't you? Are you afraid? Pray: "God, you said you have not given me the spirit of fear. You told me not to worry, but to pray and I will have peace. God, I choose peace over fear and worry. Thank you." Are you needing direction? Pray, "Lord, I need to know what you want me to do. You said "Trust in you with all my heart and not trust in myself and what I think I know. I'm looking for your landmarks." Understand

"Are you needing direction? Pray, "Lord, I need to know what you want me to do."

friend, God's Word is His will. Understand what He means about healing, and then ask His will to be done in that unhealthy situation. He doesn't lie or fail. We fail to understand what He means sometimes. Get an understanding, then apply the Word to your situation. It's better than praying your words only right? Use the Word! It will get the job done. You will get an answer. He promised, "It will accomplish what I please, It will not return to me void."

◆◆◆◆◆◆◆◆◆◆◆◆◆◆◆◆◆◆◆◆

Prayer

Dear Lord, you said whomever shall call upon your name shall be saved. I call on you today because I need you to guide and direct me. I believe everything you say. Help me where my faith is weak. I trust you. I love your Word because it's true. I love you too!

WEEK THIRTY-THREE

Are You Handling Your Power Correctly?

Scripture

Luke 12:48 " From everyone who has been given much, much will be demanded; and from the one who has been entrusted with much, much more will be asked."

◆◆◆◆◆◆◆◆◆◆◆◆◆◆◆◆◆◆◆◆

I learned something a few years ago. The reward for doing a good job for God is MORE WORK. More work leads to more responsibility. In the movie Spider Man, Peter Parker was told by his uncle Ben that he needed to be careful how he used his power. He told him that with great power comes great responsibility Friend, we all have a level of power. There is someone who looks up to us. There is someone who is depending on us. There is someone who needs our help. If you have the power to help, use it. If you have the power to lead, use it. If you have the power to love, and you do, use it. We all want to be blessed, but do we all want the responsibilities that come along with being blessed? To be blessed is to be empowered with more of what you didn't have before. If you don't handle your power (blessings) the right way, they could turn out to be a curse on your life. We are blessed to bless others.

◆◆◆◆◆

"God holds us responsible for the way we use the power He has given us."

◆◆◆◆◆

You are already blessed. Can you read this email? That's power. Can you type? That's power. Do you have a job? That's power. Do you have a voice? That's power. Can you drive? That's power. Can you breathe? That's power. Now that you see all the power you have, what are you doing with it to help others? To whom much is given much is required. God holds us responsible for the way we use the power He has given us. Now that you know you are powerful instead of powerless, ask God to show you how to use your power more effectively for Him. Your greatest blessing could come by you using effectively what you already have. Think about that friend. Moses had one stick. That one stick turned into a snake, brought water from a rock, and parted the Red Sea to help millions of people survive. What's your stick with great power. Ask God to show it to you, anoint it with His Holy Spirit's power, and get ready for your life to have a little more excitement than usual. Got Power? Use it for God and use it for Good!

◆ ◆ ◆ ◆ ◆ ◆ ◆ ◆ ◆ ◆ ◆ ◆ ◆ ◆ ◆ ◆ ◆ ◆ ◆ ◆

Prayer

Dear Lord, please forgive me for not using all the power you have given me the right way. Help me to see who I influence and lead them in the right way. Reveal to me what power you have given me, then anoint it so I can use it for your glory. In Jesus' name I pray, Amen.

WEEK THIRTY-FOUR

What Do You Need to Finish?

Scripture

John 17:4 NKJV "I have glorified You on earth . I have finished the work which you have given Me to do."

◆◆◆◆◆◆◆◆◆◆◆◆◆◆◆◆◆◆◆◆

I was riding down the street today, and my 62-year old father called me on my cell phone from his cell phone. That alone is a miracle in itself. You see, my father has never had a cell phone before in his life. My siblings and I just recently upgraded my father and mother from the answering machine to call notes. When I finished talking with him, I reflected on the joy in his voice. He was like a little kid calling his buddy about his new toy car. About two weeks ago, I went to his graduation from seminary where he was valedictorian of his Masters Degree Program. Oh, by the way, he received his Bachelors Degree in Biblical Studies as well on that same day. It's like he's a kid again. Why am I telling you my business? It's not just to tell you. My father finishing college after almost 44 years gave him a sense of fulfillment. It gave him a sense of completion. Now, He's ready to go get a Doctorate. Jesus was saying in our verse today that He

◆◆◆◆◆

"If it be your will, when I make this first step, give me the strength to finish so I can glorify you on another level."

◆◆◆◆◆

has done all that He set out to do on earth to glorify God. What do you need to finish? There are some things we cannot undo, but the ones we can, we must make time to for. Fill out the application, make the phone call, enroll in the fitness center. Don't wait 44 years to do what you can make preparations for now. Be able to look at yourself and say "Even if I don't finish, I'm going to give it my best." Then you can look up to the Lord and say, "If it be your will, when I make this first step, give me the strength to finish so I can glorify you on another level." Write down what you need to finish when you finish reading this, then write the day you're going to make the first step to get started. There's a little kid in you that wants to come out and play and call your friends to show them your new toy too!

◆◆◆◆◆◆◆◆◆◆◆◆◆◆◆◆◆◆◆

Prayer

Dear Lord, help me fulfill all that I am supposed to do on this earth. I want to leave here empty. I want to glorify you with my life. Help me be able to stand and say like your Son Jesus, "I have finished the work which you have given Me to do." Create the environment where I can get the information and support to finish. God, help me have the motivation to get started. In Jesus name, Amen.

WEEK THIRTY-FIVE

Not Yet!

Scripture

Philippians 3:13-14 "Brethren, I do not count myself to have apprehended; but one thing I do, forgetting those things that are behind and reaching forward to those things which are ahead, I PRESS TOWARD the goal for the prize of the upward call of God in Christ Jesus.

◆ ◆ ◆ ◆ ◆ ◆ ◆ ◆ ◆ ◆ ◆ ◆ ◆ ◆ ◆ ◆ ◆ ◆ ◆ ◆

Friend, if you don't get that defeated mentality out of your mind I'm going to have to come across the screen and shake you out of it! How far have you come? Too far to quit now! So what, you failed. Are you going to lie there and let the devil, doubt, and fear of failure again keep you from trying again? Paul tells us in this verse that there are some things you are going to have to PRESS your way through. When you begin to change the way you think and go when you don't feel like it, you send a letter to the devil to show up in the courtroom of your situation to testify that, " I had them confused, defeated, and heart broken, but they began quoting something about 'Pressing forward' and 'No Weapon' or something. That's when I figured they were saying to me, 'NOT YET'." Let the devil know

◆ ◆ ◆ ◆ ◆

"If Jesus left you alive for another day, He still believes in YOU!"

◆ ◆ ◆ ◆ ◆

that you're not going to give up yet. Let yourself know that you're not going to give up yet! But first let God know that you believe He can help you through on your way to your goal. NOT GONNA GIVE UP YET! NOT GONNA THROW IN THE TOWEL YET! NOT YET! Why not? You have more life ahead of you than you do behind you! If Jesus left you alive for another day, He still believes in YOU! What are you going to do with HIS support? Quit NOW? NOT YET! Go tell the devil you changed your mind about giving in!

◆ ◆ ◆ ◆ ◆ ◆ ◆ ◆ ◆ ◆ ◆ ◆ ◆ ◆ ◆ ◆ ◆ ◆ ◆

Prayer

Dear Jesus, thank you for believing in me. Help me see me like you see me. Help me see my situation like you see it. Thank you for having my back even when I didn't want to continue moving forward. Help me to complete what you started in me. Get the glory in my life. I'm not going to quit yet, so show me the next move to make. In Jesus name I pray, Amen

WEEK THIRTY-SIX

Are You a Wolf or a Sheep?

Scripture

Matthew 7:15-20 "Beware of false prophets who come disguised as harmless sheep, but are really wolves that will tear you apart."

◆ ◆ ◆ ◆ ◆ ◆ ◆ ◆ ◆ ◆ ◆ ◆ ◆ ◆ ◆ ◆ ◆ ◆ ◆ ◆

Isn't it a shame that everyone who gets close to you isn't close to you for the right reason? This text teaches us that there are people who look like they have your best interest in mind, but really will "tear you apart." This is not a word to make you paranoid, but just to put you on guard. Be careful when people try to get close to you too soon. They usually have an agenda. When I was growing up we used to have rats that would come at a certain time of the year. (I lived in the country okay!) My father would get some good cheese and set it out for them on a trap. They thought they were getting a deal, a bargain, a gift, a grand opportunity, and right when they committed to get the cheese SMACK!! They saw that it was a trap but they found out too late because they were being led by their desires and never noticed the trap. They were so focused

◆ ◆ ◆ ◆ ◆

"God is trying to show you the sheep in your life and the wolves dressed as sheep."

◆ ◆ ◆ ◆ ◆

on the cheese that they never saw the trap. Friend, you may be reading this today because God is trying to show you the sheep in your life and the wolves dressed as sheep. There's usually one person who really means you no good. Ask Jesus about Judas! Ask God to reveal to you who it is. Then ask Him how He wants you to handle that situation. Jesus simply let Judas hang himself. That's what wolves usually do if you don't fall to their level, or even panic when you discover them. Give a fool enough rope and he will hang himself.

◆◆◆◆◆◆◆◆◆◆◆◆◆◆◆◆◆◆◆

Prayer

Dear Jesus, I thank you for the protection you have given me from my enemies. I ask that you reveal to me who is for me, and who is against me. Then I pray that you have mercy on them and change their heart before your judgment comes upon them. Thanks for protecting me with "Touch not mine anointed and do thy prophet no harm." Dear Lord, forgive them for they know not what they do. Help me see what you see, then handle them like you would handle them. In Jesus' name I pray, Amen.

WEEK THIRTY-SEVEN

Believe in Jesus

Scripture

Matthew 13:58 NKJV "And He did not do many mighty works there because of their unbelief."

Jesus was not able to show out like he wanted to in His hometown, like he could away from home. He couldn't give them all that He so earnestly desired. Why? They thought they knew Him too well. They had seen Him do things before, and thought that was all he could do. They knew Him as homeboy and Mary's son, James' brother. They did not recognize Him as the Great I Am, The Great Provider, The Great Healer, The Living Water. Friend, be careful not just to know Christ as Savior and not know Him as Lord. To know Him as savior means He saved your soul. If all you know Him to do is save your soul, then that is limiting His power in your life. To know Him as Lord is to submit to His every word because Lord means He's a ruler, a king, and every other high office you

"Do you need a breakthrough emotionally, financially, spiritually? Well, Lord Jesus is in town and waiting for you to call Him by the name you need."

can think of. That means He has the power to fix any situation, and He isn't running low on supplies. Do you need a breakthrough emotionally, financially, spiritually? Well, Lord Jesus is in town and waiting for you to call Him by the name you need. Jehovah-Jireh (Provider), Jehovah-Raphah (Healer), Jehovah-Shaloam (Peace). He is either Lord of all or not Lord at all. He has a great miracle waiting for you. Will you obey Him? Then believe!

◆◆◆◆◆◆◆◆◆◆◆◆◆◆◆◆◆◆◆

Prayer

Dear Lord, I recognize you to be the ruler of all creation. You are so powerful and caring. You created the sun, moon, and the stars. How great you are! Since you did such great miracles with those large objects, I know my problem is not a problem for you. I believe you can handle any situation I have. Help me where I'm weak in believing. In Jesus name, AMEN!

WEEK THIRTY-EIGHT

Why Worry?

Scripture

Matthew 6:31-34 "So don't worry about having enough food or drink or clothing. Why be like the pagans who are so deeply concerned about these things? Your heavenly Father already knows all your needs, and he will give you all you need from day to day if you live for him and make the kingdom of God your primary concern. So don't worry about tomorrow, for today will bring its own worries. Today's trouble is enough for today."

◆◆◆◆◆◆◆◆◆◆◆◆◆◆◆◆◆◆◆◆

Why do we worry? Simply put, we forget what God can do, or we have done something wrong and fear that He won't do for us what we need. Listen friend, God loves you and wants you to be at peace and to have peace. If you've done something wrong but have a need, ask Him to forgive you of the sin. Repentance is asking God to forgive you because you offended Him. It is not asking God to forgive you just because you got caught. If you haven't sinned and you're worried, then understand that worry is a sin in itself. When you're worried, you can't enjoy the things in front of you because you're too busy worried about what bill is not paid, or what man or woman you won't have this weekend. Get a grip, friend. Change your focus. Think about what bills

◆◆◆◆◆

"You haven't really lived until you see what you can live without."

◆◆◆◆◆

are paid, think about the friends you have had, think about what you do have. What do you have right now? Thank God for it. Enjoy your day…you'll never see it again. When you close your eyes tonight, get in your bed, look back over your day and say, "I worked through that problem, I'm still alive, and God is still on the throne." Don't let worrying about tomorrow rob you of today!! Jesus knows what you need. If it's food, shelter, clothing, He says He has your back. Many times we don't need what we think we need. We just want it! You haven't really lived until you see what you can live without. When you see you can have joy without it, when you get it again, you will know the true value of it. Read Matthew 6:19-34 and change your attitude about life this day. Refuse to worry!! Trust God to know what He's doing.

◆◆◆◆◆◆◆◆◆◆◆◆◆◆◆◆◆◆◆◆

Prayer

Dear Father, forgive me for even having a hint of worry in my heart. I do have needs, and you said you will supply them. Thank you for not being a liar, but a faithful God. Thank you for always providing because I know, I don't deserve it. Thank you for the things I do have. I appreciate them. Most importantly, I appreciate you. In Jesus' name, Amen!

WEEK THIRTY-NINE

One Day at a Time

Scripture

Genesis 1:1,8 "In the beginning God created the heavens and the earth ... And God called the space "sky". This happened on the second day."

◆ ◆ ◆ ◆ ◆ ◆ ◆ ◆ ◆ ◆ ◆ ◆ ◆ ◆ ◆ ◆ ◆ ◆ ◆ ◆

When God went to work, He had a lot to do. He had a whole world to create. On the second day, He made the sky. Is anything you have to build or do bigger than a sky or world? Now, He could have done it all at once, Right? Yes He could have. But He didn't Why? Maybe it's because He wants us to see that when you take time to develop each stage, each part, each detail, the end result will be more beautiful, and will last longer. We so often try to get everything done at one time or in one day that we rush through one project to get to the next. That's not the way God works, so why do you? I know you're saying, "That's just the way my job is here in Corporate America." So what! If you are a Christian, God says, we are in the world not of the world. He says in Romans 12:1-2 "Be not conformed to this world." He's basically saying that the reason you may be so stressed is because you're functioning with a worldly mindset. Are you mad enough yet, or should I continue? Your job, your relationship, whatever it is that you want completed, will be stronger if it takes longer. If you want it weak, then it will only take a week. Sure your boss wants things done fast. By all means,

◆ ◆ ◆ ◆ ◆

"If you want it weak, then it will only take a week."

◆ ◆ ◆ ◆ ◆

get them done. But remember that God provided the job for you. He wants His children to be at peace, not always in pieces due to stress and threats of being fired. He wants you to be patient in building that relationship, not missing warning signs because your emotions were driving you too fast. You ask, "How can I slow down when so much is being demanded of me?" There is a difference between things that are urgent and things that can wait. Things that are urgent need to be done now. Things that can wait are just that, they can wait. Look at your life today and do an outline of what is urgent and what can wait. Organize your day or the rest of the week as such. That will give you peace, and help you be more patient. Even when the boss is getting on your nerves, you can have peace. Now if you have been procrastinating, you still can use that formula, but expect a little tension. God allowed it so you will be reminded not to continue procrastinating in that area. One day at a time. One assignment at a time. One phone conversation at a time. One date at a time. One thing at a time. Read Ecclesiastes 3 for a better understanding. There may be some things you need to let go of that are causing you this extra stress that you don't need. If it's not urgent and can wait, it may need to go. Your peace of mind depends on it.

◆ ◆ ◆ ◆ ◆ ◆ ◆ ◆ ◆ ◆ ◆ ◆ ◆ ◆ ◆ ◆ ◆ ◆ ◆

Prayer

Dear Jesus, forgive me for not being patient like you. I need your kind of patience in my life. I want everything you bless me with to last. So help me be patient in building it. Help me be patient with people, friends, and myself. Most importantly, help me do one thing at a time so I can be more focused, and use my energy wisely and more effectively. Thank you Jesus. In Jesus' name I pray, Amen.

WEEK FORTY

Do You Know How to Recognize God's Voice?

Scripture

I Samuel 3:10 "And the Lord came and called as before, "Samuel! Samuel!" And Samuel replied, "Yes, your servant is listening."

◆◆◆◆◆◆◆◆◆◆◆◆◆◆◆◆◆◆◆◆

Samuel was called three times by God. Yet, He didn't recognize His voice until the third time. God spoke to him audibly. God speaks in several different ways. Do you think He has been talking to your? There are five ways that He may be calling or speaking to you. God speaks through His Word the Bible, through other people, through circumstances, through dreams, through visions, and audibly. How do you know it's God? If it is God, there will always be a scripture or biblical principle to back up what He said. If it is from God and it concerns you and another individual, He works and speaks to both individuals at the same time. For instance, if someone says that God said that you are going to marry them, then God should have told you the same thing. Yes, He speaks through other people, but even if He does speak through them, what they say should agree with what God has spoken to you. Otherwise, it is not God. This may be a situation where your emotions become God and you get confused. Don't worry. He will

◆◆◆◆◆

"He speaks through other people, but ... what they say should agree with what God has spoken to you."

◆◆◆◆◆

tell you when it's time for you to make a decision through His Word. Just ask Him and He will. Is God telling you to do something and you know it's Him? Then you'd better get to doing what He said before you miss your greatest blessing ever. It probably won't make sense, and you probably don't feel you are adequate enough for the thing He's calling you to do. Well, my friend, you're not adequate enough. That's the smartest thing Moses ever said to God. After he recognized that, God said in essence, "You can't, but I can do it through you if you allow me to. I called you, so I know what it takes to get the job done. I don't make mistakes!" Like our scripture today, Samuel had a willing heart to hear and do what God says. That's all God needs from us (our availability). Once He has our attention and our willing spirit, we can part a Red Sea! Get with the program, listen and submit friend. There's a Red Sea to part!!! And He wants to use little ole' you to do it. Yeah, YOU!!! YOU!!! YOU!!!

◆ ◆ ◆ ◆ ◆ ◆ ◆ ◆ ◆ ◆ ◆ ◆ ◆ ◆ ◆ ◆ ◆ ◆ ◆

Prayer:

Dear Lord, I ask that you speak to me. I want to hear you clearly. Remove any distractions that may be hindering me from hearing you clearly. I can't do what you're calling me to do myself. I may even be a little afraid. But you said, "I can do all things through Christ who gives me strength." So since you said that, I trust you. I'm willing. In Jesus Name, Amen.

WEEK FORTY-ONE

Keyboard Praise!

Scripture

Psalm 100:4-5 "Enter into His gates with thanksgiving, and into His courts with praise. Be thankful unto Him, and bless His name. For the Lord is good; and His mercy is everlasting, And His truth endures to all generations."

◆◆◆◆◆◆◆◆◆◆◆◆◆◆◆◆◆◆◆◆

You're bored right? You're frustrated right? You're in a good mood right? If you're all three, then you really must be crazy!! Stop taking your life so seriously and smile. You may have only one good tooth. Brush that tooth and put a brace on it and thank the Lord for that tooth! Now smile and show the world why you don't have to spend as much money on toothpaste as everyone else. There's a blessing in a tooth. Crazy, huh? Life is all about how you look at it. Look at that keyboard again and let's see God at work. (Enter) "Enter into His gates with thanksgiving." Why should I be thankful? Because if I have a house, those are His gates. If I have an apartment, those are His gates. The building I work in belongs to Him too, so those are His gates. Thank Him for them. Why? (Delete) When you accepted Christ as your savior, your leader, He deleted all your past sins. (Insert) Not only did He delete your sins, He inserted Himself into your life so

◆◆◆◆◆

"(Insert) Not only did He delete your sins, He inserted Himself into your life so you could live with Him forever!"

◆◆◆◆◆

you could live with Him forever! (Backspace) Now that you have a relationship with Him, when you sin, He can hit backspace when you confess your sins to Him and change your ways...(I John 1:9). (Up Arrow, down arrow, side arrows) He wants to give you direction for your life. Remember, He inserted Himself in so He knows where to go if you let Him lead. (Control) That brings us to letting Him have complete control of your circumstances and your life. (Shift) That means the power has to shift from your hands to His. (Home) You can have assurance that all of this is true, and relax here on earth and not let life get to you because you know He has a home for you that is not like any other you've seen. Now before you leave me, remember this...when you finish reading this push (SAVE) because that will remind you that Jesus can save you from any situation. It's all about how you look at it! (Escape) Now I'll make my escape! (End)

◆◆◆◆◆◆◆◆◆◆◆◆◆◆◆◆◆◆◆◆

Prayer

Dear Lord, I thank you and praise you for everything I have, and I thank you for the things I thought I needed but you didn't let me have. I praise you, and I am thankful for the gift of life. You have kept things from happening to me when I knew something bad should have happened. You have given me things when I knew I didn't deserve them. Now that I look at it, I'm just glad to be alive because, I don't deserve to be! Thanks Lord. You're the greatest. This smile is for you. I Love You!

WEEK FORTY-TWO

Don't Quit!

Scripture

2 Kings 13:18-19 "Now pick up the other arrows and strike them against the ground." So the king picked them up and struck the ground three times. But the man of God was angry with him. "You should have struck the ground five or six times!" he exclaimed. "Then you would have beaten Aram until they were entirely destroyed. Now you will be victorious only three times."

◆◆◆◆◆◆◆◆◆◆◆◆◆◆◆◆◆◆◆◆

King Jehoash was facing a problem and a situation that he had no clue how to defeat. Have you ever been there? He had a problem that just would not go away? Have you ever been there? He was given instructions to strike the ground with some arrows, but he wasn't given a particular amount of times that he should strike the ground. What does that have to do with me? How many times have you tried to start your business, work through that relationship, finish school, get out of debt, regain self-control? God says strike the ground! That means pray, keep trying, keep going, don't stop until you get it going or get

◆◆◆◆◆◆

"Your life is not a game of baseball. It's not three strikes and you're out! Keep Swinging!! Keep Swinging!! God ain't through yet so keep trying!!"

◆◆◆◆◆◆

out of it! Don't stop after the third time like the king did. Maybe he stopped at three strikes because he was frustrated. Your life is not a game of baseball. It's not three strikes and you're out! Keep Swinging!! Keep Swinging!! God ain't through yet so keep trying!! Don't Quit!

◆◆◆◆◆◆◆◆◆◆◆◆◆◆◆◆◆◆◆

Prayer

God, I ask that you give me a spirit of determination. I ask that you show me which way to go. I ask that you strengthen me to go where you want me to go. Show me what's your will and what's not. When I see your will, help me fulfill it. Help me to keep striking!! In Jesus name, Amen

WEEK FORTY-THREE

Deal With It!

Scripture

Exodus 14:15 "And the Lord said to Moses, "Why do you cry to me? Tell the children of Israel to go forward. But lift up your rod, and stretch out your hand over the sea and divide it."

◆◆◆◆◆◆◆◆◆◆◆◆◆◆◆◆◆◆◆◆

Does there seem to be anything from your past trying to catch up with you to destroy your future? Have you experienced doubts in your mind on whether or not you can get past your current situation? Do you feel the pressure caving in around you? Do you feel trapped? Moses did. So did the children of Israel. They knew where they had come from was so close to them that they could smell them. They knew they couldn't win against what had them in bondage before on their own. Moses did too. So they complained to Moses. Moses cried to God, and God replied, "Deal With It!" In essence he was saying, "Don't you know I brought you this far for a reason?" I see what you can't defeat. I see your situation. As a matter of

◆◆◆◆◆

"And Moses cried to God. And God replied "Deal With It!" In essence he was saying, "Don't you know I brought you this far for a reason?"

◆◆◆◆◆

fact, I set it up for you. Now I've already equipped you with what you need to go to the next level. That's right, a stick. I gave it to you a long time ago. You've had it all this time. Now take your stick, take your prayer, take the faith that you do have and believe in Me, and believe in yourself. I know it doesn't look like much and it's not. But when you stretch it out, I'll give it miraculous power. Now is not the time to turn back to your old ways of thinking. Now is not the time for quitting. I've got your back. Let's keep on moving forward. There's more ahead of you than behind you! What's in front of you will change if you keep moving forward. Remember, I've got your back. Trust Me!

◆ ◆ ◆ ◆ ◆ ◆ ◆ ◆ ◆ ◆ ◆ ◆ ◆ ◆ ◆ ◆ ◆ ◆ ◆ ◆

Prayer

Dear Lord, forgive me for doubting you. Give me the strength to trust that you wouldn't bring me this far to leave me hanging. I trust you. Let's go forward together. I'll deal with what's facing me and let you deal with what's behind me. I love you Jesus. In Jesus name, Amen!

WEEK FORTY-FOUR

Do You Really Know You?

Scripture

Jeremiah 17:9-10 "The human heart is most deceitful and desperately wicked. Who really knows how bad it is? But I know! I the Lord search all hearts and examine secret motives. I give all people their due rewards according to what their actions deserve."

◆◆◆◆◆◆◆◆◆◆◆◆◆◆◆◆◆◆◆◆

I often quote the phrase, "I know me." After reading this scripture, after looking at some decisions I've made in my life, after looking at some things I've done that I said I would never do, after examining some thoughts that I have thought, and after reading this scripture, God reminded me that I don't really know me like I think I do. But you know what, He said He does. Have you ever said, "God knows my heart?" If you have, you need to understand that He really knows your heart. He knows when you mean what you say, why you do what you do, and why you don't do what you were supposed to do. He says our hearts are not just wicked, but deceitful and desperately wicked; that our heart is so deceitful that we can deceive ourselves! Ask God today why you are going to make the decision

◆◆◆◆◆

"Do you really want to know? Ask God today to show you who you really are."

◆◆◆◆◆

you're going to make. Why are you with the person you're with? Why do you want to have the kind of job, man, woman, house, clothes, vehicle that you want? Ask Him to really show you . Your motives may be off, or they may be right on target. Do you really want to know? Ask God today to show you who you really are. Only He knows us truly. We lie to ourselves because we want to see only the good. Measure who you are, compared to Christ, not man today and see how well you're doing. He's waiting on you so He can tell you who you are. Just ask! He loves you enough to tell you the truth. Are you pleasing people, yourself, or God? If you please Him, then He'll take care of the other two. Don't you know God loves you? He just wants the best for you, that's all, THE BEST! Don't settle.

◆ ◆ ◆ ◆ ◆ ◆ ◆ ◆ ◆ ◆ ◆ ◆ ◆ ◆ ◆ ◆ ◆ ◆ ◆

Prayer

Dear Lord, show me my motives in my choices today. I want to have the right motives. I want only what you want for me, because only that will bring fulfillment. You know me; please help me get to know you. In Jesus name I pray, Amen.

WEEK FORTY-FIVE

Get Your Smile Back!

Scripture

Psalm 27:13 "Yet I am confident that **I will** see the Lord's goodness while I am **here** in the land of the living.

◆◆◆◆◆◆◆◆◆◆◆◆◆◆◆◆◆◆◆◆

The holidays are coming, and you've had a stressful year. You are starting to miss that mother who is no longer alive. You miss the spouse that you are now divorced from. You miss that child that God allowed to go to heaven earlier than expected. You wonder what Christmas and Thanksgiving is going to look like financially. You try to fight these feelings off, but they seem to want to dominate your mind more and more each day. What do you do? Feel all of the emotions that come to you! Begin talking with God and letting him know how you feel. Then thank Him for the opportunity to love and be loved. Don't feel guilty, because that doesn't change a thing but your mood. It's okay to feel lonely; just don't **embrace** your loneliness. Now after you've had a good cry or good spell, open your mouth and say, "Lord thank you for allowing me to have another day to live. I love you so much. I don't deserve to live, but I'm thankful for your love and patience with me. I may be hurting now, but I will see more of your goodness while I am yet in the

◆◆◆◆◆

"Smile like you know who loves you more than anything!"

◆◆◆◆◆

land of the living. Thank you for providing all of my needs in advance. Thank you for knowing everything that concerns me." Friend, ask God to show you what life really is all about this holiday season. I guarantee you will see His goodness to you....more than you will be able to handle. **Fight through your negative emotions.** You have so much life, **good life**, ahead of you. After all you've been through, it can't get anything but better! If it's been good, it can't get anything but **GOODER! (Smile, you look and feel better when you do!)** ***You really gain appreciation for sunshine after a real good storm!*** God's Son, Jesus, shines **in your storm** and shows you the way out! **Smile** like you know who loves you more than anything!

◆◆◆◆◆◆◆◆◆◆◆◆◆◆◆◆◆◆◆

Prayer

Lord, give everyone joy in their life today that will sustain them through life. Help us see situations through your eyes. Thanks for always being there for us. Amen.

WEEK FORTY-SIX

Fear Factor

Scripture

Psalm 23:4 "Even when I walk through the dark valley of death, I will not be afraid, for you are close beside me. Your rod and staff protect and comfort me.

◆◆◆◆◆◆◆◆◆◆◆◆◆◆◆◆◆◆◆◆

Have you seen the show Fear Factor? If you haven't, it's about 4 individuals who do daring and sometimes disgusting things in order to win a prize at the end of the show. One show had an aquarium full of small nonpoisonous snakes with plums at the bottom of the tank. Each participant had to dive head first into the tank, and using their mouth, put as many plums from the bottom of the tank into a bucket beside the tank. Whomever had the most would win that phase of the game and move to the next level. Whoever quit or did poorly would sometimes scream in their fear of snakes and would not complete that level. Friend, living life is sometimes like Fear Factor. Some things you want you have to face things you fear the most to get there. Are you fearing being lonely the rest of your life? I know you want to get through the holidays, but you may not have that "special someone" to share them with. Listen

◆◆◆◆◆

"When you don't go places because of what you know you will have to deal with but you really need to go, you die that day"

◆◆◆◆◆

friend, Christmas and Thanksgiving may feel like your fish tank full of snakes, but remember not to let the poisonous snake bite of depression sink into your spirit. Dive in anyway and thank God for the family and friends and peace of mind you have. Don't fear going home. Don't fear being alone. Don't sit up looking crazy all by yourself. We have to go through the valley of the "shadow of death." That's all these times are... shadows of death. Depression wants to be your best friend this holiday season. Do you want to be friends with it? If not, begin writing down all the things you have in your life today. Then, thank God for them. You have less to fear and more to be thankful for than you thought. Make it through this season being thankful for real. Get a head start on seasonal drama. You have a game of life to win! God's got your back.

◆ ◆ ◆ ◆ ◆ ◆ ◆ ◆ ◆ ◆ ◆ ◆ ◆ ◆ ◆ ◆ ◆ ◆ ◆ ◆

Prayer

Father, I pray for all who have some fears to face. I pray that since they have to face them, that they will have the strength and courage to go through it with you. I claim joy for your people instead of sadness. I pray that you give them people who love to be around them also. I pray that others find new friends that are good for them. I pray that singles will not compromise during this time of year, but think clearly and not make decisions based on their emotions. I pray all these things in Jesus' name, amen.

WEEK FORTY-SEVEN

Who Killed Jabez?

Scripture

I Chronicles 4:10b "Oh that you would bless me and extend my lands..."

◆◆◆◆◆◆◆◆◆◆◆◆◆◆◆◆◆◆◆

Are you in need of a blessing? Well, I haven't heard about the Prayer of Jabez in a minute. It's as if he was a fad or something. No friend, that is found in the **Bible.** We have to be careful of thinking that certain scriptures are fads. If it worked the first time you prayed it, why wouldn't it work now? Somebody has tried to kill Jabez! Jabez was not a fictional character. The book he is found in is not a comic strip or tabloid paper. No friend. This man was found in the word of God. He's not Jesus, but his prayer went to God. It is a model of how we should cry out to God when we feel there is more to life than where we are. It's not saying we are greedy or not thankful. When we ask for more, we simply are saying we want all God has for us. Do you want all He has for you? Then be faithful and thankful for what you have and then ask for some more to be thankful for and to share with others. Well,

◆◆◆◆◆

"Pray your prayer for increase and watch God move! Ask and it shall be given..."

◆◆◆◆◆

if you like being unemployed, making the same money you've been making since 1991, having more bills than money, being single with no prospects, then you just keep your mouth closed! But if you believe God is a God who wants you to increase, He wants you to depend on Him and then He'll show the world what he can do for His kids. You ought to open your mouth and say **BLESS ME INDEED!** Jabez is dead, but you're not. God is not. Your ability to ask is not. The prayer he prayed is not. Pray your prayer for increase and watch God move! Ask and it shall be given...

◆◆◆◆◆◆◆◆◆◆◆◆◆◆◆◆◆◆◆◆

Prayer

Dear Lord, for everyone who wants more in their life, I ask that you bless them with a supernatural surprise. Bless them and meet every need above and beyond what they expected. In Jesus' name I pray, AMEN!

WEEK FORTY-EIGHT

The Hand of the Lord

Scripture

I Chronicles 4:10 ".......that your hand would be with me...."

The hand of the Lord is described in the Bible meaning different things. It can mean His power (right hand) or it can mean His anointing. Jabez is praying that the Lord's hand is with Him in everything he does. This is an excellent prayer to pray. If you really want God to work in every area of your life you need His anointing. What is that? You need special ability to endure situations and produce fruit. Whatever God touches through you will be different than anything that He doesn't touch. Your work will be different, your smile will be different, your prayer will be different, the way you handle situations will be different, and your attitude will be different. The anointing of God (His hand upon you for a certain cause) will overcome when everything else crumbles. The hand of God also means His blessing. You don't want any job, house, relationship, or anything without God's bless-

"Sin drains the power out of your life. God doesn't like getting His hand dirty with it, so He removes it until you repent and become clean."

ing. Those things soon fade away, or give you more trouble than you can take. Ask God what things He is not blessing in your life. He'll show you, and He'll show you why. Then either get rid of it, or ask Him to show you how to make it right. You want His hand on everything you do. Sin drains the power out of your life. God doesn't like getting His hand dirty with it, so He removes it until you repent and become clean. Yeah you still have your relationship, but you can't feel His touch or His power like you need to. Don't you want to be closer than where you are now? Ask Him to have His hand destroy the thing that's keeping you dirty. He'll do it so you can enjoy His blessing on your life.

◆◆◆◆◆◆◆◆◆◆◆◆◆◆◆◆◆◆◆◆

Prayer

Dear Lord, forgive me of any area of my life where I'm dirty before you. I need your hand to be with me. I ask that you forgive me, cleanse me, and now be with me greater than ever before; that I may stay in your will, and fulfill your will. Thank you Lord. In Jesus name I pray, Amen

WEEK FORTY-NINE

Are You to Scared to be Blessed?

Scripture

I Chronicles 4:10 "Oh that you would bless me indeed, and enlarge my territory, that your hand would be with me, and that you would keep me from evil, That I may not cause pain."

◆◆◆◆◆◆◆◆◆◆◆◆◆◆◆◆◆◆◆◆◆

Now I know that I consider myself to be a pretty brave brother. I love God. I want His best for my life and the life of others. I also must admit that God has truly been good to me. Things are going at a blessed pace for me. The tripped out part about it is, I haven't really been asking God for much. Yet, He has been giving me more than I could imagine. That brings me to this point. When I first began praying the prayer of Jabez, soon after I was hired at Friendship-West, I began leading more people than I've ever been responsible for, having more resources financially and opportunities that I never had before. I didn't pray that I would get this position; I prayed that God would give me all that He has for me. Truthfully, I never imagined it would feel like this. Sometimes, God will bless you to where it will make you nervous. You feel like you can't take anymore. Jabez was saying in his prayer, "God, bless me until I get nervous!" Why would you get

◆◆◆◆◆

"Are you afraid for God to really bless your socks off? Start being obedient to His will..."

◆◆◆◆◆

nervous? You realize that you didn't do it, and if it gets any better or bigger you can't do it unless God works in you. Are you afraid for God to really bless your socks off? Start being obedient to His will, and then ask Him to bless you. Ask Him to bless you to do more for Him. If you do more for Him, He can do more for you. I guarantee you that if you ask God to show you where you need to get your life right with Him, and you take the step toward obedience, then God can use you for more than what you are doing now. He'll bless you so until you feel you're being set up for something! Do you dare to repent, and submit, and ask God to INCREASE your life and those it affects? Are you scared? You don't deserve it anyway. Why not ask? Pray this prayer below every time you turn your computer on and watch God begin to use you for a greater cause for His glory not yours.

◆◆◆◆◆◆◆◆◆◆◆◆◆◆◆◆◆◆◆

Prayer

Oh, that you would bless me, enlarge my territory, your hand be with me and keep me from evil, so I will not cause myself or anyone else pain, but bring joy to my life and those I come in contact with. Thanks Jesus. Amen.

WEEK FIFTY

What's Up With My Mouth?

Scripture

James 3:7-10 "People can tame all kinds of animals and birds and reptiles and fish, but no one can tame the tongue. It is an uncontrollable evil, full of deadly poison. Sometimes it praises our Lord and Father, and sometimes it breaks out into curses against those who have been made in the image of God. And so blessing and cursing come pouring out of the same mouth. Surely my brothers and sisters this is not right!"

◆◆◆◆◆◆◆◆◆◆◆◆◆◆◆◆◆◆◆◆

I really don't have to say anything else do I? When you opened your mouth this morning, what were the first words that came spewing out? Before you read this email, what were you saying? How many people have you talked about today? How many people have you encouraged today? That tongue is something else isn't it? We have so many reasons for the things we say, but the reality is we enjoy saying what we say. If you don't have anything good to say, please don't poison someone else's spirit with the venom of your tongue. So many "Christians" would be in prison serving a life sentence if we were tried for how many murders we committed by talking behind someone else's back about them. We down

◆◆◆◆◆

"You have a choice today. You can use your tongue for Mess or to Bless!"

◆◆◆◆◆

others because it makes us feel bigger. Ask yourself today why you say the things you say, and see if God agrees with you. If you are talking about one of His children, I don't think He will. If you are trying to hurt someone's feelings, I don't think He will. If you are talking to someone else and not confronting and talking with your fellow Christian brother and sister about a problem you have with them, I don't think He will. What comes out of your mouth tells what you feel about God and yourself. Even a fool is considered wise until he opens his mouth. The only reason we should speak is to edify or build up someone. Have you done that today? Have you thanked God for your life today? You have a choice today. You can use your tongue for Mess or to Bless! Your choice shows your maturity.

◆◆◆◆◆◆◆◆◆◆◆◆◆◆◆◆◆◆◆◆

Prayer

Dear Lord, forgive me of any sins I've committed with my tongue. Help me use it to bless you and others and to build your kingdom. In Jesus name, Amen.

WEEK FIFTY-ONE

Is This You Lord?

Scripture

Matthew 14:28 Then Peter called to him, "Lord, if it's really you, tell me to come to you by walking on the water."

◆◆◆◆◆◆◆◆◆◆◆◆◆◆◆◆◆◆◆◆

Is there anything you've been praying about? Are there situations in your life where you wonder like Peter, "Is this the Lord or what?" We find here in Matthew 14 that Jesus came walking on the water to the boat of the disciples at 3 a.m. in the morning. They were afraid, because they knew Jesus, but they had never seen him in this way before. Friend, could God be trying to show you something in a way that you have never seen Him before? That may be the reason you can't sleep right at night. The next time you can't sleep, open your mouth and say, "Lord, are you trying to reveal yourself to me in a way that I didn't even imagine? Help me see you and not what I think I need to see." And when He answers you, in order for you to receive what He is trying to get to you, you will have to walk on the water with Him. Basically, you're going to have to do something you didn't think you could do in order to get what you never have had before. If it's from

◆◆◆◆◆

"If it's from Jesus or is Jesus, when you move toward it you won't sink as long as you keep your eyes on Him."

◆◆◆◆◆

Jesus, or is Jesus, when you move toward it, you won't sink as long as you keep your eyes on Him. God is trying to get you out of your boat friend. It's time to step out.

Before you step out of the boat:

1. Ask God if this is him or not.

2. Wait for Him to give you an answer (Begin to journal every sermon you hear, scripture you read until you get a Biblical answer) It may take a week or more, maybe even a day.

3. Get out of that comfortable mindset or situation and get to Walking in Faith when you get your answer!!!!

Things from God don't always come like we expect them to. Don't put God in a box. He's an out of the box kind of God. It may not make sense, but that doesn't mean it ain't God as long as if accomplishes His will in your life.

◆ ◆ ◆ ◆ ◆ ◆ ◆ ◆ ◆ ◆ ◆ ◆ ◆ ◆ ◆ ◆ ◆ ◆ ◆ ◆

Prayer

Lord, help me to keep an open mind to what you can do. You can do anything. Help me to be patient and trust that you know what I need and what I am trying to do. Give me wisdom to recognize you even if I have never seen you a certain way before. In Jesus' name I pray, amen.

WEEK FIFTY-TWO

Happy New You!

Scripture

Matthew 9:17 "And no one puts new wine into old wineskins. The old skins would burst from the pressure, spilling the wine and ruining the skins. New wine must be stored in new wineskins. That way both the wine and the wineskins are preserved."

◆ ◆

My Pastor, Frederick D. Haynes III, made an astounding observation after his New Year's Message a year ago. He stated, "You can't have a Happy New Year unless you have a Happy New You!" That is what I have come to share with you today friend. Do you want this year to be one where you make forward progress? That means you're going to have to get some new wineskins in order to have new wine placed in you. What is a wineskin? A wineskin was an animal that was killed, had his head cut off and sewn together to be filled with new fermented wine in Biblical times. When the wineskin was new, it was flexible, pliable, and able to handle the fermenting, changing structure of the wine inside. When the skins were old, they could not handle new wine because they were brittle and useless. What kind of old wineskin thinking do you need to change this year? What

◆ ◆ ◆ ◆ ◆

"God can't fill you with His Holy Spirit to give you a new way of thinking until you choose to submit to Him."

◆ ◆ ◆ ◆ ◆

kind of old wineskin choices do you need to avoid making? What kind of old wineskin relationships do you need to get rid of? God can't fill you with His Holy Spirit to give you a new way of thinking until you choose to submit to Him and say this: "Not what I want, but what you want this year for me God." When you say that, you're well on your way to experiencing a Happy New You. Remember, "Greater is He who is in you than he who is in the world!" Become flexible this year with God. Become a willing vessel this year for God to use you however he pleases. Make a resolution to have More of God. If you have more of God, God will have more of you. You can have all of God in you if you will just submit more to His way of thinking this year. Pray more, fast more, give more, love more, trust God more, forgive more, and you'll be happier more. Now that's what makes a Happy New You!

◆ ◆ ◆ ◆ ◆ ◆ ◆ ◆ ◆ ◆ ◆ ◆ ◆ ◆ ◆ ◆ ◆ ◆ ◆

Prayer

Dear Lord, I want to know you more this year. I want the wine of your Holy Spirit to fill and control me more. From this day forward, I will make a better effort to do exactly what you say, and not what I want. If you don't help me I'll mess up this year like last year. I need your help. I love you Jesus! Amen.

Notes:

Notes:

Notes:

Notes:

Additional Tools for Christian Education by

Rev. Marcus D. King

Warning Signs

What is Friendship Dating?

A Real Woman

Unpacking Your Emotional Baggage

Stay Focused

Don't Be Unequally Yoked!

It's Time to Settle Down

Complete Faith

Making a Godly Choice

Is Your Mate a Trick or a Treat?

Control Your Tongue

How to Handle Temptation

Can't We All Get Along?

The titles listed-above are available on Audiocassette Tapes at $5.00 USD each. Please send your order and a check or money order payable to Rev. Marcus D. King to the address listed-below. Add $2.00 for shipping and handling. ($1.00 for each additional tape)

Donations to help advance the ministry are accepted.

For additional information and speaking engagements, please send all correspondence to:

M.D. King Ministries | P.O. Box 398306 | Dallas, TX 75339-8306
Email: mdkministries@hotmail.com